"*The Anxious Thoughts Workbook for Teens* presents a comprehensive, approach for managing negative thoughts in a way that is engaging, relatable, and easily accessible by adolescents. Written by one of the world's clinical and research experts in the field, and drawing on an extensive clinical and research evidence base, this workbook is an excellent resource for adolescents, parents, and clinicians."

—**Maja Nedeljkovic, PhD**, associate professor at Swinburne University of Technology in Australia; director of the Swinburne Psychology Clinic; and coeditor of the book, *The Self in Understanding and Treating Psychological Disorders*

the anxious thoughts workbook for teens

cbt skills to quiet the unwanted negative thoughts that cause anxiety & worry

DAVID A. CLARK, PHD

Instant Help Books
An Imprint of New Harbinger Publications, Inc.

Publisher's Note

INSTANT HELP, the Clock Logo, and NEW HARBINGER are trademarks of New Harbinger Publications, Inc.

New Harbinger Publications is an employee-owned company.

Distributed in Canada by Raincoast Books

Copyright © 2022 by David A. Clark
Instant Help Books
An imprint of New Harbinger Publications, Inc.
5674 Shattuck Avenue
Oakland, CA 94609
www.newharbinger.com

Cover design by Amy Shoup

Acquired by Ryan Buresh

Edited by Kristi Hein

Library of Congress Cataloging-in-Publication Data on file

Printed in the United States of America

24   23   22

10   9   8   7   6   5   4   3   2   1   First Printing

Contents

letter to the reader

Dear Reader,

Welcome to *The Anxious Thoughts Workbook for Teens*. No doubt you bought this book, or it was given to you, because anxiety is causing problems in your life. Do you feel that you get more anxious than your friends or others in your family do? Do you find that anxiety comes at the worst times, causing you more distress? Maybe you feel alone because you're so anxious around your peers, or you're not doing as well as you'd like in school because of your anxiety.

If anxiety has become a problem in your life, this workbook is for you.

It's very normal to feel anxious. In fact, mild anxiety can be helpful. If you're mildly anxious about an upcoming exam, it can motivate you to study harder. But if the anxiety is too severe, you can feel so upset that you avoid studying altogether, with predictable results. When anxious feelings become severe and cause us to act in unhealthy ways, it's time to do something about them.

The Anxious Thoughts Workbook for Teens shines a spotlight on severe, unhealthy anxiety. It focuses on anxious thoughts and how they're responsible for making your anxiety worse. You'll learn that anxiety often begins with a negative thought that spontaneously pops into your mind. We call these *unwanted intrusive thoughts*. They're often related to what's happening in our life. When we assume the thoughts are true and try hard to push them from our mind, they get worse, driving up our anxiety. Once the anxiety gets severe, we avoid the situations we think trigger the anxiety. This is how anxiety becomes a problem.

In this workbook you'll find activities that can reverse this anxiety process. You'll learn how to challenge your anxious thoughts, and you'll discover new, healthier ways of thinking about your anxiety and its triggers. I'll show you the limits of mental control and how acceptance can turn anxiety on its head. The last module takes you beyond anxiety, where you'll learn how to use *positive* intrusive thoughts to boost your happiness.

You'll probably find some activities more helpful than others. I encourage you to try all the activities and then repeat the ones you find most effective. You might find the workbook more helpful if you do it with a parent or counselor. Wherever you are in your search for freedom from anxiety, I believe you'll find this workbook helpful. You've taken an important first step. Now I invite you to read on and discover how to calm your anxious mind.

—David A. Clark, PhD
November 2021

PART 1

The Runaway Mind

1 sticky thoughts

for you to know

You know what it's like to have sticky hands. But did you know your thoughts can be sticky too? Upsetting thoughts, images, or memories that pop into our mind can be especially sticky. Often, once they get into our head, we can't stop thinking about them. You might try different strategies to clear your mind, just like feeling the urge to wash your sticky hands. But the harder you try to stop thinking the upsetting thought, the more you think about it.

We call these *negative intrusive thoughts,* and they can make us feel anxious, depressed, guilty, or frustrated.

Any thought can be intrusive, but here are some particularly common ones:

- *Maybe I hurt my best friend's feelings, and now she's mad at me.*

- *I acted like such a jerk, and everyone's talking about it.*

- *I really blew that exam—how could I be so stupid?*

- *I'm such a loser; no one really likes me.*

- *I'm different from everyone else.*

When these types of thoughts suddenly pop into our mind without any effort, we tend to assume they must have special significance. This is what makes them so hard to get out of our mind. And sticky thoughts tend to keep coming back.

But if you take the time to understand your own sticky thinking, you can start to change these patterns.

for you to do

The next time you feel upset, write down the unwanted sticky thought that popped into your mind and wouldn't leave.

My sticky negative intrusive thought: _____

_____

When you're feeling upset, it's really hard to be aware of what you're thinking. But it's important to train yourself to catch these unwanted negative thoughts, because they're the rocket fuel of your distress. And the stickier and more repetitive the negative thought, the greater its pull on your emotions. Over the next week or so, focus on times when you're upset and see if you can discover any negative intrusive thoughts that stick in your mind. You can write them down here.

Another sticky negative thought: _____

_____

Another: _____

_____

Another: _____

_____

Are you surprised that certain negative thoughts get really stuck in your mind, while others pop into your head and are no big deal? You'll learn that how you understand the intrusive thought (its personal significance) and whether you try to control it (try to not think about it) determines how long it stays in your mind.

more for you to do

Sometimes our sticky thoughts become so frequent and repetitive that they turn into obsessions. Think of the distressing thoughts that often flood your mind. Then place a checkmark (√) beside the statements that describe your experience with sticky intrusive thoughts.

1. _____ *The same thought, image, or memory pops into my mind over and over.*

2. _____ *It's very difficult to get the intrusive thought out of my mind.*

3. _____ *The intrusive thought makes me feel more upset or distressed.*

4. _____ *I really don't want to have the intrusive thought.*

5. _____ *I've developed certain rituals to deal with the intrusive thought, like washing, checking, redoing, rereading, or reordering.*

6. _____ *I realize the intrusive thought is extreme or even ridiculous.*

7. _____ *I get stuck on the thought and can't think of anything else.*

If you checked several statements—especially numbers 1, 2, and 5—your sticky thoughts could be obsessive. The activities in this workbook will be helpful, but note that obsessions are a particularly sticky form of thinking. You'll need to give yourself extra time for the workbook activities. If you are seeing a therapist, tell them your findings from this exercise. If you're reading this workbook on your own and you suspect you might have obsessive-compulsive disorder (OCD), talk to your parents and consider contacting a mental health professional. There are specific treatment strategies that are highly effective in reducing obsessive thinking.

for you to know

Sticky thoughts are often pretty negative, making us feel anxious or upset over the smallest thing. And sticky thoughts often pop into our mind quite suddenly—and once they're there, it's hard to get rid of them. Think of their sudden appearance as a *mental invasion*. A thought, image, or memory can sneak into your mind, and before you know it, a wave of sadness, anxiety, or fear washes over you.

Remember, any thought, image, or memory can be an unwanted mental intrusion. These often deal with issues that matter most to us, like what our friends think of us, our relationships with parents and siblings, how well we're doing in school, our future, our physical appearance, romantic relationships, sexuality—the list goes on. And because these intrusions happen spontaneously, we tend to believe they must be true.

Let's look at what your mental invasions tend to look like—and how they might be fueling feelings of anxiety, frustration, guilt, or depression.

for you to do

Take a moment to review the three or four sticky negative thoughts you wrote down in Activity 1. Now write one negative thought that sticks in your mind when you feel upset.

My upsetting (sticky) negative thought: _____

_____

Next, use the following scale to rate how well the six statements describe your experience of the negative thought.

Statements	Not Relevant	Somewhat Relevant	Very Relevant
The thought pops into my mind on its own; I don't have to try to bring it to my mind.			
The thought is very undesirable; I don't like it when I think this way.			
The thought grabs my attention, and I can't think of anything else.			
It's hard to concentrate once I start thinking like this.			
The thought is very upsetting.			
The thought is difficult to control; I can't get it out of my mind no matter how hard I try.			

How well did these statements describe your experience of negative thinking? Consider whether these statements are relevant for other types of negative thoughts you have.

If negative thoughts often pop into your mind, grab your attention, and are difficult to control, then mental intrusions might be driving your anxiety and distress.

more for you to do

If you haven't discovered the most important intrusive thoughts responsible for your anxious or depressed feelings, don't give up. When you're feeling upset, it's only natural that all your attention is focused on the feeling. It can be hard to capture that first thought that popped into your mind and got you upset. You'll have other chances in this workbook to become more aware of unwanted intrusive thoughts. Meanwhile, try this next exercise to improve your *intrusion detection skills*.

Jessica noticed that she often felt anxious when she tried to connect with her friends. Looking closer, she realized the first thought that popped into her mind was always *They're probably thinking I'm pathetic, no fun, and boring.* This mental intrusion could easily make Jessica feel anxious about her friends.

Over the next week, notice times when your mood suddenly changes. Maybe you're doing something and almost instantly become frustrated. Or while alone in your room, listening to music, you feel a wave of sadness. Or while studying for an exam or practicing for an upcoming concert, suddenly your stomach starts churning, which you know is anxiety. Ask yourself, *What just went through my mind?* Write the thought in your journal or the notes app on your phone.

After you've done this a few times, consider your list of intrusive thoughts. Do you see any themes in these mental invaders? Write them down below.

My Recurring Negative Intrusive Thoughts

_____

_____

_____

_____

_____

3   connect the dots

for you to know

You want to feel better. You're seeing that changing how you think can really help. And to do that, you'll need to become skilled at catching *the unwanted intrusive thoughts* that suddenly invade your mind and lead you down the rabbit hole of distress. This is hard, because they happen quickly—in a fraction of a second.

Maybe you're wondering how you can catch unwanted intrusive thoughts if they're so sudden. Fortunately, there's a tight connection between our thoughts and feelings. And we're naturally more aware of how we feel than what we are thinking, so you can work back from the emotion to discover the intrusive thought that made you feel bad in the first place. We know certain types of thoughts occur with certain feelings. Here are some common feeling-thought connections.

Feeling		Thought
Sadness	⟷	Thoughts of loss or failure (*I'm such a loser; I deserve nothing*).
Fear	⟷	Thoughts of danger (*I could get seriously hurt, even die*).
Anxiety	⟷	Thoughts of possible threat, helplessness (*I'm a total stranger at this party*).
Anger	⟷	Thoughts of unfairness (*This is unfair; I'm being treated badly*).

for you to do

Discovering your feeling-thought connections is an important step toward control over anxiety. In this activity, you'll learn to use a Feeling-Thought Record to begin making these connections. (A downloadable version of this worksheet, along with other free tools, is available at http://www.newharbinger.com/48787; see the back of the book for more information.) Over the next week or two, use this form to write down what you're thinking, seeing, or remembering when feeling anxious, sad, frustrated, or guilty. You can also write in your journal or on your phone's notes app.

Start catching your thoughts by writing down what's happening at the time you feel anxious or upset. In the Situation column, note where you were, what you were doing, and who was with you. In the Feeling column, note what you're feeling: sad, anxious, frustrated, angry, guilty, annoyed, irritated, and so on. If you're feeling several emotions (which we often do), circle the most intense emotion.

The Negative Thoughts column is the most important. Ask yourself *What just went through my mind? What am I thinking about that at this moment?* Focus on your thoughts and describe these. After listing several negative thoughts, circle the first thought that went through your mind.

Feeling-Thought Record

Situation	Feeling	Negative Thoughts

Were you able to capture the negative thinking connected to your distress? Learning to be more aware of the thoughts that make us feel anxious or depressed is a basic skill taught in cognitive behavioral therapy (CBT). At first it may seem weird to be asking yourself, *Okay, I'm feeling anxious, so what am I thinking?* But changing your negative thinking is the key to overcoming emotional distress like anxiety.

more for you to do

If you had difficulty catching your negative intrusive thoughts, take a look at Rachael's Feeling-Thought Record. Notice how her first thought led her down a mental rabbit hole ending in anxiety and frustration.

Example: Rachael's Feeling-Thought Record

Situation	Feeling	Negative Thoughts
1. Studying for math exam	Uptight Frustrated Irritated	No matter how hard I try, I'll never understand this algebra. – I'm hopeless when it comes to math. – Why am I so stupid? – I'm going to fail this exam and then fail my math course.
2. Get text about Derek's party on the weekend	Anxious	I hate parties; they make me feel so uncomfortable. – I don't want to go; I'll make up an excuse. – I'm such a boring person; no wonder I have no friends.

Notice how Rachael's pattern of negative thinking makes her frustrated and anxious about math and parties. The first thought that pops into her mind is a negative thought about the present situation.

After seeing this example, try again to capture the negative thinking related to your times of feeling anxious and upset.

4 we're in this together

for you to know

Everyone has unwanted, negative thoughts pop into their mind. In fact, most people occasionally have quite disturbing intrusive thoughts, some of which you might consider disgusting or immoral. If you find this hard to believe, try doing the survey in the next exercise.

for you to do

Select four or five close friends or family members to take the Negative Intrusions Survey. Make sure you choose people you can trust who'll be honest and understand your struggle with anxiety. Introduce each to the survey by saying:

Have you ever had a negative or upsetting thought, image, or memory suddenly pop into your mind for no reason? You don't want the thought, you find it upsetting, and you'd like to stop thinking about it, but it's hard to get it off your mind. Maybe the thought seemed to come from nowhere and now it's in your mind.

If the person confirms this, ask them to tell you about their thought and how it made them feel. Later, write their name and the negative intrusive thought in the following worksheet. (A downloadable version is available in the free tools at http://www .newharbinger.com/48787.)

Negative Intrusions Survey

	Name of Friend/ Family Member	Negative Intrusive Thought, Image, or Memory
1.		
2.		
3.		
4.		
5.		

Did everyone you surveyed report at least one negative intrusive thought? Chances are at least some of them have had thoughts of this kind. Are you surprised to learn your mind is not so different from others'?

If someone you talked to denied having unwanted, distressing mental intrusions, ask if they'd be willing to track their thoughts over the next couple of days to see if they have negative intrusions but hadn't realized it. Some people aren't aware of their negative thoughts because they quickly forget about them. The thoughts aren't important, so they don't pay attention to them. They can be surprised at how negative their thinking can be when they keep a record of their spontaneous thoughts.

more for you to do

So you've learned that everyone has unwanted negative thoughts. But you may wonder, *Why do I have more distressing intrusive thoughts than most people? Doesn't this make me different from everyone else?* There are many reasons why some people have many negative intrusive thoughts and others have few. Maybe you're going through an especially difficult time, or you tend to be more emotional. Also, some people have a natural tendency to be more aware of their spontaneous thinking. Being able to "think about thinking" can be a positive characteristic. We'll call these people *intrusive thinkers.*

If you're wondering whether you have a natural tendency to have more negative intrusive thoughts, take the Intrusive Thinker Test. (A downloadable version is available at http://www.newharbinger.com/48787.) Place a checkmark (√) beside the statements that apply to your experience of intrusive thinking.

Intrusive Thinker Test

☐ *I'm a creative person; I often have a different way of seeing things.*

☐ *I've had disturbing things happen to me.*

☐ *I have significant personal problems or issues.*

☐ *I often feel anxious, depressed, or upset.*

☐ *I'm an emotional person.*

☐ *I often overanalyze or overthink stuff.*

☐ *I have difficulty controlling unwanted thoughts.*

If you checked three or more statements, it's possible you're an intrusive thinker. This doesn't mean you have to live the rest of your life in misery. You can learn to tame this unwanted negative thinking and tune in to the more positive thoughts that come from the creative side of your brain.

If you're an intrusive thinker, make sure your goals are realistic. Be kind and patient with yourself as you make your way through this workbook. With your rich supply of intrusive thoughts, you'll want to spend more time on the more challenging activities.

Whether you're an intrusive thinker or not, your goal is the same: to lower the frequency and intensity of anxious thinking. It's not realistic to think you'll completely eliminate all negative thoughts. The workbook activities are designed to help everyone struggling with anxiety learn better ways to deal with negative thinking. So help is on the way, whether you're a high or low intrusive thinker, or somewhere in between.

5 discover your creative mind

for you to know

You have an amazing brain. And however much you might dislike your negative intrusive thoughts, this kind of thinking is an important part of it! Neuroscientists have discovered that 50 percent of our thinking involves spontaneous thoughts that pop into our mind without any effort or guidance on our part.[1] Unwanted mental intrusions are just one example of this kind of thinking, which includes daydreaming, mind wandering, and fantasizing. In fact, spontaneous thinking is so common it's actually been called the brain's default mode of operation.[2] So spontaneous intrusive thoughts are the normal way our brain functions.

Our ability to think spontaneously is important for our very survival. *Positive intrusive thoughts* help us solve personal problems and be creative. If we could, we'd all choose to have only positive intrusive thoughts. But that's not possible. When you're a creative, intrusive thinker you'll have both positive and negative intrusive thoughts.

So the goal isn't to stop negative intrusive thoughts (if that were even possible) but to *harness your intrusions*. You'll learn to dampen down the effects of unwanted distressing intrusions and boost the benefits of positive spontaneous thought.

Have you been so focused on negative thoughts and feelings that you've forgotten the upside of your positive spontaneous thoughts? Maybe intrusive thinking is a more positive force in your life than you realize. Our ability to think creatively depends on the brain circuits that make spontaneous thought possible. So if you are an intrusive thinker, congratulations! You have an amazing mental ability. Your challenge is to manage it wisely.

---

1   K. Christoff, "Undetected Thought: Neural Determinants and Correlates," *Brain Research* 1428 (2012): 51–59.

2   M. A. Killingsworth and D. T. Gilbert, "A Wandering Mind is an Unhappy Mind," *Science* 330, no. 6006 (2010): 932.

for you to do

Let's take a break from negative mental chatter and use an exercise to discover the positive—even creative—mental intrusions you're experiencing every day. How often does an idea suddenly come to you that solves a tricky situation or problem in your life? Imagine you're trying to learn a complicated math or science concept, and you don't get it. Suddenly a solution comes to mind, and now you understand. When that happens, thank your creative, intrusive thinking mind.

Over the next week or two, use the Creative Intrusions Diary to catch times when a positive, creative, or inspirational idea suddenly pops into your mind. In the left column, write down the situation, circumstance, or problem that you faced. It could be a school problem, a situation with your friends, or a disagreement with your parents or siblings. In the right column, write down the sudden, unexpected thought or idea that gave you better understanding or a solution to the problem. (A downloadable version is available at http://www.newharbinger.com/48787.)

Creative Intrusions Diary

Situation, Circumstance, or Problem	Creative Problem-Solving Intrusive Thought

What did you discover about your creative brain? Are you surprised at how often intrusive thinking actually helped you deal with a problem, circumstance, or difficult situation? Intrusive thinking is not always bad—it can help solve difficult problems in our lives.

more for you to do

If you're still struggling to discover positive intrusive thoughts, ask a family member or close friend to help you list your good ideas. Discuss how you came up with some good ideas for boosting your athletic training, improving your music or art skills, raising your school grades, or dealing with friendship or family problems. Write these down below.

A. My Good Ideas for Sports, Music, or Art

    1. _____

    2. _____

B. My Good Ideas for Raising My Grades

    1. _____

    2. _____

C. My Good Ideas for Improved Relationships with Friends, Parents, or Siblings

    1. _____

    2. _____

After making your lists of good ideas, circle the numbers of the ones that came to you spontaneously. These good ideas just popped into your mind, and you thought *Brilliant! That's exactly what I need to do.* They are positive intrusive thoughts, courtesy of your creative brain.

PART 2

Explore Your Mind

6 the white bear experiment

for you to know

How much control do we have over our mind? I'm sure you've experienced being bored in school, your mind wandering far from what's happening around you. A wandering mind can relieve boredom or be a little annoying—or it can be a serious problem, like when you're writing an exam and your mind keeps drifting off to an irrelevant topic. You realize you're wasting valuable exam time, but you feel helpless to control your distracting thoughts.

We all experience these failures in *mental control*—the ability to pay attention to wanted thoughts and to ignore unwanted thoughts.

At the heart of mental control is one of its greatest mysteries: the *mental control paradox*. Let's say a disturbing thought pops into your mind, like *I wonder if Jason is cheating on me.* You don't want to be thinking this way, because it upsets you. If it stays in your mind, you'll probably end up confronting Jason, leading to an argument. If this happens repeatedly, it could result in a breakup—the very thing that scares you most. So you try to push the jealous thought out of your mind, but the harder you try *to not think about Jason cheating*, the more you think about Jason cheating. The more important this thought you're trying *to not think* and the more emotionally upsetting the thought, the greater the paradoxical effect, because the more effort you put into suppressing a thought (trying to not think about it), the stronger its pull on your attention. It's a simple equation:

Greater Mental Effort = Less Mental Control

for you to do

If you have some doubts about the limits of mental control, try doing *the white bear experiment.*

Don't Think About the White Bear

Find a quiet place where you can sit comfortably without interruption. Close your eyes, take a couple of slow, deep breaths, and relax. After a minute or two of relaxation, read these instructions, then follow them.

Set the stopwatch on your phone to two minutes. Now try to not think about a white bear. *Try as hard as you can to prevent any thought of a white bear from entering your mind.* If the thought of a white bear pops into your mind, place a checkmark in the text boxes provided below and gently turn your attention to any thought except the white bear. Stop the experiment after two minutes, count the checkmarks, and complete the two ratings below.

Total number of white bear intrusions: ☐ ☐ ☐ ☐ ☐ ☐ ☐ ☐ ☐ ☐ ☐ ☐

1. How well did you keep the white bear thought out of your mind? Circle:

    0 = not well at all   1 = moderately well   2 = very well

2. How much effort was needed to *not think* about the white bear? Circle:

    0 = no effort   1 = moderate effort   2 = great deal of effort

Did you have only a few checkmarks or quite a few? Did the white bear keep popping back into your mind despite your best effort? If so, you just experienced the mental control paradox. Most people who try the white bear experiment are surprised by its difficulty. Its relevance for anxiety is clear. The harder you try to not think about something you're anxious about, the more you'll think the anxious thought. Remember the mental control equation when you're doing the activities in the rest of the workbook.

more for you to do

Maybe the white bear experiment has made you question whether you have less mental control than other people. To find out, try the white bear experiment on a couple of friends or family members. Choose people you can trust, who will be honest and take the experiment seriously. (Cheaters and jokers not wanted!)

Repeat the experiment with each participant, having them raise their hand to signal when the white bear thought intrudes. Keep track of these intrusions. Then have each participant complete the self-ratings on success and effort.

How did your results compare with your participants'? Did they find it just as hard as you did to suppress the white bear thoughts? What's important is not the specific number of checkmarks but learning just how difficult it is to stop yourself from thinking an unwanted thought. In fact, the harder you try to not think about something, the more you may think about it. We'll be using this finding in the rest of the workbook to show you a more effective way to deal with your anxious mind.

I don't want to think like this

for you to know

You've learned that our mental control is limited. We all have unwanted intrusive thoughts that pop into our mind and make us anxious. These thoughts stick in our mind because the harder we try to not think about them, the more we think about them. This means that minds are often inefficient; they can even work against themselves! Let's see why this happens by considering Samantha's story.

Samantha (Sam), a first-year university student, had always been shy and nervous around strangers. For Sam, the most frightening part of starting university was talking to other students in her class and residence. Her social anxiety began with an intrusive thought like *You're going to feel anxious; people will notice it and think you're a bore and pathetic*. Sam tried hard to stop dwelling on these anxious intrusive thoughts. She tried to convince herself that she'd be okay, but the thoughts wouldn't go away. The only solution seemed to be keeping to herself and avoiding all social activities.

When we're anxious, certain types of unwanted thoughts stick in our mind. If you assume yours must be important because you keep thinking about them and they make you upset, you'll try hard to get them out of your mind. Once this happens, you're falling into the *mental control paradox*. This can lead to other forms of negative thinking like worry, rumination, and even obsession.

Let's consider the thinking behind Sam's social anxiety. She gets a tweet announcing a Friday night party in her residence. Sam's anxious mind kicks into full gear:

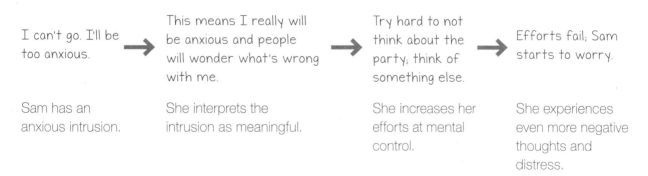

I can't go. I'll be too anxious. →	This means I really will be anxious and people will wonder what's wrong with me. →	Try hard to not think about the party; think of something else. →	Efforts fail; Sam starts to worry.
Sam has an anxious intrusion.	She interprets the intrusion as meaningful.	She increases her efforts at mental control.	She experiences even more negative thoughts and distress.

Ultimately, Sam's problem is in engaging with the intrusive thought, which magnifies it and leads to more anxiety and worry.

for you to do

Now that you've seen how Sam's way of thinking increased her social anxiety, explore how engaging with your anxious thoughts makes *you* more anxious. These questions focus on different ways you might give your anxious thoughts more significance than they deserve. You can come back and change your answers later if needed.

1. List two anxious intrusive thoughts that frequently pop into your mind. (Hint: Look at the sticky thoughts you listed in Activity 1.)

   _____

   _____

2. Why do you think these thoughts are so important to you? (Hint: Maybe you think they reveal your true character, or you're afraid they mean something bad will happen to you.)

   _____

   _____

3. What do you think will happen if you don't stop thinking like this?

   _____

   _____

4. What other negative thoughts are you having because of the anxious intrusive thoughts?

   _____

   _____

more for you to do

Most thoughts that pop into our mind don't upset us. Every day we have intrusive thoughts that are so unimportant we can't even remember having them. Why do only certain thoughts make us anxious, while the rest come and go with little influence on our emotions?

It depends on how we deal with the thoughts.

You can learn a lot about your mind by considering your normal way of dealing with the intrusive thoughts that don't upset you. Sam would sometimes have an intrusive thought of her parents separating and how this would affect her life. Notice how she was able to calm herself by not engaging with the anxious thought about her parents.

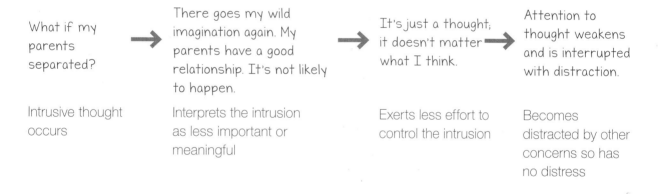

List two intrusive thoughts that frequently pop into your mind that are not distressing. (Hint: Look at the creative intrusions you listed in Activity 5.)

_____

_____

_____

1. What makes these thoughts so unimportant? (Hint: Maybe you think they're irrelevant, or you're not concerned about any consequences.)

    _____

    _____

    _____

    _____

2. Are you able to let the thoughts come and go in your mind? Why does it matter so little whether you have the thoughts in your mind or not?

    _____

    _____

    _____

    _____

anxious intrusions diary 8

for you to know

When you're anxious, it's easy to get focused on how you feel. It's almost impossible to ignore the uncomfortable sensations, like muscle tension, a churning stomach, nervousness, and a racing heart. But the way we think also has a big effect on anxiety. Usually an upsetting thought pops into our mind, which then kick-starts the anxious mind. Some earlier activities introduced you to this idea of *anxious intrusive thoughts*. These first thoughts are especially important in understanding why your anxiety increases with some but not with others. It's important to get better at catching these intrusive thoughts so you can deal with the anxiety early before it gets out of control.

for you to do

To calm your anxious mind, you need to identify your anxious intrusive thoughts. The best way to improve your anxiety detection skills is to get into the habit of writing down the anxious thought when it occurs.

The Anxious Intrusions Diary is a good way to keep track of your anxious thoughts. (A downloadable version is available at http://www.newharbinger.com/48787.) In the first column, briefly describe the situation that made you feel anxious. It could be something at home, your friends, school, sports, or your health. In the next column write all your anxious thoughts about that situation. Then circle the thought you believe was the first anxious thought. That will be your *anxious intrusive thought*. In the third column, write what you tried to do to reduce the anxiety or stop it altogether. In the first row you'll see an example based on Jarrett, a high school student who had intense test anxiety.

Anxious Intrusions Diary

Anxious Situation	Anxious Thoughts	Anxious Response: Coping Strategies
Jarrett's Example: Studying late at night before a physics exam; struggling to understand certain problems.	What's wrong with me? Why can't I get these practice problems right? I can't do well on this exam unless I know everything. I should be able to figure this out. I must be stupid; this was explained in class. I'm going to really blow this exam. I'll end up barely passing the course, which will make it almost impossible to get into my first-choice college.	Kept trying to solve the practice problems late into the night to prove I could do them. Got very emotional and vented my frustration with my parents. Eventually gave up and tried to sleep. (None of these strategies helped; I just got more anxious.)

Anxious Situation	Anxious Thoughts	Anxious Response: Coping Strategies

Most often the anxious intrusive thought will be the first thought, image, or memory that pops into your mind when dealing with the anxious situation or concern. Notice that Jarrett's intrusive thought (*What's wrong with me? Why can't I get these practice problems right?*) led to other anxious thoughts, like predicting he'd blow the physics exam and end up with a poor mark, which would lower his grade point average and chances for admission to his first-choice university. Anxious intrusive thoughts are important because they fire up our anxious mind. If you learn to deal with the first anxious thought, you'll be able to stop the anxiety from getting out of control.

more for you to do

Make copies of the Anxious Intrusions Diary so you can use it whenever you experience intense anxiety. It should take you only a minute or two to write down the anxious thoughts when they happen. If that's not possible, make a brief note of the anxiety experience. At the end of day, recall your anxiety experiences and write down the anxious thoughts that went through your mind. If you have difficulty knowing what you are thinking when anxious, start by remembering what you *felt*.

You learned in Activity 3 that sadness, fear, anxiety, and anger have their own unique thought contents. The same is true for other emotions. We feel frustration when we think our progress toward a goal is being blocked, guilt when we think we've done something wrong, and shame when we think we've embarrassed ourselves so badly that others will think we're worthless. (For more about feeling-thought connections, see the free tools available at http://www.newharbinger.com/48787.)

It's important to know how you think anxiously. By using the Anxious Intrusions Diary, you'll get better at tracking your anxious thoughts, especially the first one that pops into your mind. If you have trouble figuring out what you think when you're anxious, list all the emotions you feel along with the anxiety, then search for thoughts that go with each emotion.

a matter of importance   9

for you to know

Our brain is constantly active. Thoughts fill our mind every waking minute of the day. This means that our brain must sort through thousands of thoughts to determine which are most important for living a happy, productive life. We assign each thought a level of importance, and the more important the thought, the more attention we give it.

But the brain is not perfect. We often give higher importance to thoughts that don't deserve it—or lower importance to healthy thoughts. And with anxiety we exaggerate the importance of thoughts about threat and danger.

Take Samantha's anxious thoughts about talking to her peers. The thought pops into her mind *I'll be so anxious, I won't be able to stand it*. She pays a lot of attention to this thought because she believes it's an accurate prediction. But maybe the anxiety won't be as bad as she's thinking; maybe she'll do a better job at handling it. If Samantha assigned less importance to the thought, she might tell herself, *It's true I'll be anxious, but maybe I'll be able to get through this better than I think*.

for you to do

Review the intrusive thoughts you wrote in your Anxious Intrusions Diary (Activity 8). Pick one that occurs often and causes you considerable anxiety:

_____

_____

Now consider how you make this an important thought and answer the following questions.

1. Are you concerned the anxious thought has some negative effect on you, or that it could cause something bad to happen to you? If yes, describe the negative consequence here:

    _____

    _____

2. Would you blame yourself if you didn't stop this negative consequence from happening? If yes, explain what you'd blame yourself for:

    _____

    _____

3. Do you believe the anxious thought must be important because you spend a lot of time thinking about it?

    Circle: YES   NO

4. Do you believe it's important to not think about the anxious thought? If yes, explain what might happen if you lost control of the thought:

    _____

    _____

Have you been wondering why you have more anxiety than your friends? It's because you pay more attention to your anxious thoughts. Your answers to these questions explain why you consider these anxious thoughts to be so important. Anxious thoughts get sticky, and when we give them greater importance than they deserve, we can't stop thinking them, and anxiety increases. So learning how to make anxious thoughts less important is an effective way to decrease anxiety.

more for you to do

If you're still unsure how you're giving too much importance to your anxious thoughts, consider Sam's responses to the same questions:

Sam's anxious intrusive thought: I can't go to the residence party; I'll be so anxious that I won't be able to stand it.

1. **Sam's response to the first question:** Even thinking about the residence party makes me anxious. If the anxiety is this bad now, it'll be unbearable at the party. I'll totally embarrass myself.

2. **Sam's response to the second question:** Of course. It's all my fault. I should have better control over my emotions. If I make a fool of myself, it's because I didn't have a better handle on my anxiety.

3. **Sam circled NO for the third question.**

4. **Sam's response to the fourth question:** I need to stop thinking about being anxious before I can force myself to go to the party. If I'm thinking like this now, it'll make me even more anxious at the party.

Now select another anxious intrusive thought from your Anxious Intrusions Diary. Try completing the four questions again. Is your way of thinking about (that is, interpreting) your anxious thought similar to Sam's or different? Later in the workbook I'll return to this question of how we exaggerate the importance of anxious thinking and how this can make us feel anxious.

10 trying hard to not think

for you to know

Kateisha posted a crazy dance video on social media. At first she got several likes, but then someone posted a nasty comment about her dancing. Kateisha started to feel anxious, thinking that others might feel the same way about her video. She wished she'd never posted it. She ended up deleting it, but it was too late. In her mind, the damage had been done. She kept thinking *Everyone thinks I'm a loser. How can I face them?* For Kateisha, her anxious thinking about the video was extremely important. She had to face these people at school and deal with their online comments. So it makes sense that Kateisha tried hard to not think about the disastrous video. But remember the white bear experiment (Activity 6)? The harder you try to not think a thought, the more you end up thinking it. So the more Kateisha tried to not think about the video and her reputation, the more she actually thought about it.

for you to do

Are you, like Kateisha, trying hard to not think about your anxious thoughts? Write down two anxious thoughts you recorded in your Anxious Intrusions Diary (Activity 8).

_____

_____

Now respond to these questions.

1. Thinking of the two anxious thoughts, how much mental effort (concentration) do you put into trying to get them out of your mind?

    ☐ Try really hard

    ☐ Try moderately hard

    ☐ Make a slight effort

    ☐ Don't even try

2. How often do you try to control your anxious thoughts?

    ☐ Every time I have them

    ☐ Only when I'm feeling upset or anxious

    ☐ I usually don't try

    ☐ I never try; just let them come and go

Even if you try only moderately hard to not think anxiously, and you try to control your thoughts only when you're upset, you're still putting too much effort into thought control. The harder you try to not think anxiously, the more you supercharge these thoughts so they stick in your mind.

more for you to do

When upsetting thoughts pop into your mind and you're trying to not think about them, it's only natural to use certain mental strategies. We use them so often we're hardly aware we're doing it. What's important is that some strategies are more effective than others.

The following is a list of seventeen common mental control strategies. (A downloadable version is available at http://www.newharbinger.com/48787.) Think back to when you felt anxious. Next, read each item and circle YES if you probably used that control strategy or NO if you rarely used that strategy. Also rate each strategy's probable effectiveness, with 0 for not effective, 1 for somewhat effective, and 2 for very effective.

Mental Control Strategies

Control Strategy	Relevance		Effectiveness Rating		
1. Distraction; I think of something else.	YES	NO	0	1	2
2. I try to make sense of the anxious thought.	YES	NO	0	1	2
3. I criticize myself for thinking anxiously.	YES	NO	0	1	2
4. I seek reassurance from family or friends.	YES	NO	0	1	2
5. I tell myself to stop thinking anxiously.	YES	NO	0	1	2
6. I distract myself with a task I hate doing.	YES	NO	0	1	2
7. I try to figure out why I'm having these anxious thoughts.	YES	NO	0	1	2

Control Strategy	Relevance		Effectiveness Rating		
8. I look for evidence to convince myself the anxious thought is stupid.	YES	NO	0	1	2
9. I do a compulsion over and over (like checking) or repeat the same phrase so I'll feel less anxious when I have the thought.	YES	NO	0	1	2
10. I concentrate on the anxious thought to push it from my mind.	YES	NO	0	1	2
11. I let the anxious thought sit in my mind and do nothing to control it.	YES	NO	0	1	2
12. I try to turn the anxious thought into something positive.	YES	NO	0	1	2
13. I try to relax, meditate, or breathe slowly.	YES	NO	0	1	2
14. I laugh at myself, making fun of my anxious thinking.	YES	NO	0	1	2
15. I pray.	YES	NO	0	1	2
16. I tell myself everything will be okay.	YES	NO	0	1	2
17. I avoid people or situations that might trigger anxious thinking.	YES	NO	0	1	2

Take a moment to review your answers. You may be doing two things that make anxious thinking worse: trying too hard to not think anxiously, and using control strategies that are not very effective. Don't be discouraged. Most of us do exactly the same thing when we're anxious. The good news is, you've discovered two ways to reduce your anxiety: reducing your mental control effort and changing the way you deal with anxious thoughts. You'll learn how to do both in the rest of the workbook.

PART 3

Calm Your Anxious Thinking

11 stinking thinking

for you to know

A famous psychologist named Albert Ellis called negative thoughts that make us feel bad about ourselves *stinking thinking*. Your anxious intrusive thoughts are a type of stinking thinking because they make you feel weak, inferior, and scared. Thoughts like *What if I fail? What if they think I'm weird?* and *I can't do this* are all examples of anxious stinking thinking. When your thinking stinks day after day, it can undermine how you see yourself, and your self-worth takes a nosedive. You begin to think of yourself as weak, helpless, and unable to deal with life.

Isabella was a deep thinker who loved to read science fiction and paranormal stories that questioned reality and the meaning of life. Often she'd have an intrusive thought like *I wonder if life is real, or are we living in a matrix?* Sometimes she'd play with this idea, trying to convince herself she wasn't alive. But she always ended up laughing at herself and thinking *What a weird idea! I've got a wild imagination*. This was not stinking thinking, because it didn't make Isabella feel bad about herself. But when she had the thought *What if I end up alone and miserable the rest of my life because I'm so different from everyone else?* she felt anxious and helpless. It reminded her the future is uncertain. Clearly this was intrusive stinking thinking because it made her feel bad about herself.

Are you like Isabella? Do you know when your anxious thoughts become stinking thinking?

for you to do

Discover whether stinking thinking is making you anxious and harming your self-esteem with this three-part investigation.

1.   Think of a recent event where something upsetting or unpleasant happened to you—like a disappointment, an unkind remark, an argument, or a difficult task.

      Isabella's unpleasant experience: I heard that my aunt had cancer. She still has young children. Our whole family is very upset by this news.

      Write your unpleasant experience: _____

      _____

2.   When you think about this experience, what thoughts pop into your mind?

      Isabella's intrusive thoughts: We can never know whether something bad will happen in the future.

      Your intrusive thoughts about this experience: _____

      _____

3.   When you think about this bad experience, how does it make you feel? What are you thinking about yourself? Do you blame or criticize yourself?

      Isabella's example: I feel anxious and scared when I think about the future. It makes me think I have so little control over life. It causes me to think of myself as weak, fragile, and helpless.

      How the experience made you feel: _____

      _____

      _____

If your anxious thoughts in step 2 caused you to feel bad about yourself, you experienced *stinking thinking*.

more for you to do

Take a look at the anxious intrusive thoughts you wrote down in step 2 and how these thoughts made you feel about yourself in step 3. How could you think differently about your negative experience so it doesn't become stinking thinking?

Isabella's example: Everyone lives with not knowing the future. Some people I know live their life well, and others don't. This means I do have control over how I choose to live my life. I can focus on each day and live it the best way I know how.

Write how you could think differently here: _____

_____

_____

thinking about thinking 12

for you to know

Does your brain ever surprise you? Were you ever amazed that you solved a difficult math problem, wrote a song or poem, or mastered a difficult dance routine or piece of music? Our brain does something else equally amazing: we can think about thinking. That's right. You can think about something and then think more deeply about what you are thinking.

Psychologists call thinking about thoughts *metacognition*. Our brains do it all day long. We try to understand the meaning and significance of our thoughts. We might ask ourselves, *Why am I thinking about this right now? Where did that thought come from? What does it mean?* or *What should I do about it?*

Metacognition makes some anxious thoughts stinking thinking, but not others. Here's how it works: Clayton felt a strong attraction to Shanice. He suddenly thought *I should send Shanice a friend request.* But this thought filled him with anxiety. He started worrying whether he should do it. He had self-doubts. Maybe she was too good for him. This was becoming stinking thinking for Clayton. He was getting anxious and down on himself.

When Clayton thought *I should send Shanice a friend request,* he interpreted this thought as a significant threat. He started imagining what could go wrong: She might ignore his request, think he's weird or creepy, and tell all her friends. He could end up feeling embarrassed and humiliated. His thought had become stinking thinking.

for you to do

Write down an anxious thought that pops into your mind. For ideas, look back at your Anxious Intrusions Diary (Activity 8).

My anxious intrusive thought: _____

_____

_____

The next few questions about *metacognition* can help you discover how you are thinking about the anxious thought. You'll learn whether the thought makes you feel anxious because you're telling yourself the thought is a big deal—a significant personal threat.

1. How does the anxious thought cause you to think negatively about yourself? List these negative thoughts:

    _____

    _____

    _____

    _____

2. Does the anxious thought increase the chance that something bad will happen to you? If yes, what are you afraid will happen?

    _____

    _____

    _____

    _____

3. Did the anxious thought remind you of some bad experience? If yes, what was it?

_____

_____

_____

_____

4. Did you act or feel differently because of the anxious intrusive thought? Describe how the thought changed your feelings and behavior:

_____

_____

_____

_____

5. Do you think it's important to not think about the intrusive thought? Explain why:

_____

_____

_____

_____

more for you to do

Write a short paragraph that describes how you think about the anxious intrusive thought. This is your metacognition based on your previous answers. It'll explain why the anxious thought is so significant that it has become stinking thinking for you. Here's Clayton's example:

One reason I'm paying so much attention to this thought is that it makes me feel inferior. I'm convinced that thinking about the friend request so much will jinx me. It'll cause me to mess up and look pathetic if I send the request. Thinking like this is bad luck. It becomes more difficult to act natural and confident around Shanice. It also reminds me of past humiliation, like when I asked a girl to the movies and she made up a lame excuse. Thinking about Shanice takes over my mind. It gets me down, and I feel like doing nothing. It's important that I stop thinking like this. I need to get better control over myself.

My "thinking about thinking" paragraph:

_____

_____

_____

_____

_____

_____

_____

healthy anxious thoughts 13

for you to know

The previous two activities focused on unhealthy anxious thinking: stinking thinking. But not all intrusive thoughts are negative, and not all anxious thoughts are unhealthy. It depends on how we think about the thoughts. We call that *metacognition*.

Think of an event or activity where you really want to excel. Maybe it's your team making finals, a dance or music recital, a college admissions interview, or joining a fraternity. You've had intrusive thoughts about it for days, and you're nervous about the event. If your anxious thoughts were healthy, you might think:

Obviously I'm concerned about this event, because I can't stop thinking about it. Let's think about what's most likely to happen. It'll be obvious that I'm nervous, but no one will care. They'll be too focused on their own performance. In the past I've managed my anxiety in similar situations, so I can do it again.

This would be a healthy way of thinking about feeling anxious.

for you to do

This activity is designed to help you discover whether you have healthy anxious thinking.

Start by remembering some difficult or stressful experience that you got through successfully—a competition, evaluation, family issue, or relationship problem. While dealing with this experience, did anxious or worrying thoughts pop into your mind? Try to remember thoughts that made you feel a little anxious but weren't overwhelming. Write them here:

_____

_____

_____

_____

_____

_____

Next, review the following likely possibilities for how you may have convinced yourself the anxious thoughts were no big deal—that you could handle the situation. Describe what you told yourself in each instance.

1. *The thought has no influence on my future.* How did you persuade yourself that this is true?

   _____

   _____

   _____

2. *There is nothing I can do about the thought—it's all in my imagination and there's nothing to solve.* What helped to convince you this is true?

_____

_____

_____

3. *I must not try to control the thought.* How did you remind yourself to stop this effort?

_____

_____

_____

4. *This thought has no personal significance for me.* What helped you let go of that feeling that it *was* significant?

_____

_____

_____

Think back to how you interpreted your anxious intrusive thought in the stinking thinking activity. Compare your answers to the ones you provided in this activity. Can you see how the anxious thought becomes unhealthy when you think of it as a significant personal threat that you can't handle? But it becomes healthy when you think of it as less significant and something you can handle. We can use metacognition to determine how our thoughts make us feel more or less anxious.

more for you to do

You've been exploring how you make some anxious thoughts healthy. It's natural for anxious or worrying thoughts to pop into your mind before an important, stressful event. Based on your answers to the previous questions, compose a healthy thinking paragraph. Explain how you became convinced that your anxious thoughts about the stressful event were not a big-deal threat. Include statements of how you believe you can cope with the intrusive thoughts and the situation itself.

_____

_____

_____

_____

_____

_____

_____

_____

it's not a catastrophe 14

for you to know

When you get an anxious thought, do you sometimes take it to extremes and imagine something terrible could happen to you? Let's say your anxious intrusive thought is that you don't fit in with your friends. You then imagine everyone making fun of you behind your back and posting stuff about you being a loser. If this is how your anxious mind works, you can call it *catastrophizing*. When you catastrophize, your thinking becomes unhealthy and your anxiety gets much worse.

There are two big problems with catastrophizing:

- We assume the terrible outcome is more likely to happen than is realistic.

- We imagine a severe, overwhelming, worst-case possibility.

Does catastrophic thinking play a big role in your anxiety? Bad things *can* happen, and we need to be prepared for them. But catastrophic thinking is different. When we catastrophize, we think of only the very worst possibility. We also think and act like it's sure to happen. Instead of *I'll try out for varsity football and make it to the final cut,* we catastrophize *I'll try out for varsity football, be the worst tryout by far, and end up the laughingstock of the entire school.*

for you to do

Write down an intense anxious thought you recorded in your Anxious Intrusions Diary (Activity 8):

_____

_____

_____

When you had this anxious thought, did you imagine various possible outcomes? List a couple of possibilities:

_____

_____

_____

_____

_____

Look at the worst possible outcome you listed. Is it remotely possible but unlikely to happen? That's catastrophic thinking. Write it here:

_____

_____

_____

_____

more for you to do

You can learn several ways to shut down catastrophic thinking:

- Think of your anxious intrusive thought as a mildly upsetting experience.

- Make a list of less severe possible outcomes to your anxious concern.

Catastrophic thinking is a hard habit to break. But you can do it by creating a *new, less severe story* you can use when the anxiety or worry returns. Based on your catastrophic thinking examples, answer these questions:

1. Imagine three less extreme, although still undesirable, possible outcomes to your anxious concern:

   a. _____

   b. _____

   c. _____

2. Are these less extreme outcomes more likely than the catastrophe? Rate each possible outcome on a scale from 0 percent (no chance of happening) to 50 percent (50/50 chance of happening) to 100 percent (certain it will happen):

   a. _____

   b. _____

   c. _____

3. Is there any way to be less negative about the intrusive thought or even think of it more positively? Think about a situation that makes you anxious and describe how your thoughts could be less catastrophic:

   _____

   _____

   _____

With several less extreme possible outcomes imagined, it's time to put it all together. Write a new story of a less extreme possibility you could think about when feeling anxious:

_____

_____

_____

_____

_____

_____

_____

_____

Coming to believe the rewritten story more than the catastrophic one will take lots of practice, so whenever you have an anxious intrusive thought, practice rewriting and imagining a new, less extreme story. Over time you'll start to think more naturally in the less extreme way—and you'll feel less anxious.

for you to know

What you see, hear, and feel is the basis of your *reality*. Imagination is the opposite of your reality; they are two very different experiences. Knowing the difference between imagination and reality is very important to our mental health.

Anxious thinking is connected to both reality and imagination. Catastrophizing is an example of anxious thinking connected to our imagination. But anxious thoughts can also have a connection with our reality. We can get anxious about what's happening to us right now. We assume that anxious thoughts triggered by reality are more important. We're more likely to pay attention to them. When this happens, these thoughts drive up our anxiety.

Let's say you have the intrusive thought *Will I get picked on at school today?* This thought will cause you a lot of anxiety because it's connected to your daily experience. You may assume that just having the intrusive thought means there's a good chance you'll get bullied.

We all make mistakes in our thinking when it comes to anxiety. Catastrophizing is one mistake connected to our imagination. Stinking thinking is another. A third mistake is exaggerating the connection between our anxious thinking and what happens in our real world. Are you thinking that things could go wrong in your day because you've had anxious intrusive thoughts? Are you treating your thoughts like they're a prediction of bad things to come your way? Let's look at whether this happens in your imagination or in reality.

for you to do

Think back to times when you had anxious or worrying thoughts, then answer the questions that follow.

When you've had anxious thoughts pop into your mind, how often did something bad happen to you afterward? List some examples:

1.	4.
2.	5.
3.	6.

When you've had an anxious intrusive thought, how often did the bad outcome you expected *not* happen to you afterward? Provide an example:

_____

_____

From your experience, you have an anxious thought; you fear something bad is going to happen, but it doesn't. Does this mean the anxious intrusive thought is a result of your imagination?

_____

_____

This exercise is called *reality testing*. It's an effective way to reduce anxiety. You discovered that you can have an anxious thought but nothing unusual happens afterward. Psychologists often advise *Treat your thoughts like they're thoughts and not facts*. An intrusive thought of something bad happening is not the same as something bad happening.

more for you to do

Making a prediction is another way to reality test your anxious thoughts. When an anxious thought pops into your mind, write it in the left column of the worksheet. (A downloadable version is available at http://www.newharbinger.com/48787.) In the second column write down what you fear might happen. This is your prediction. Wait a couple of days, then write what actually happened. Did your prediction come true? The first row provides an example.

Anxious Predictions Worksheet

Anxious Intrusive Thought	Make Your Prediction	Describe What Happened Afterward
I'll be picked on at school today.	Axel's going to make a rude comment when I get on the bus; all his friends will start laughing and making fun of me.	The next three days I got on the bus, Axel did make a rude comment once, but everyone ignored him.
1.		
2.		

Anxious Intrusive Thought	Make Your Prediction	Describe What Happened Afterward
3.		
4.		
5.		
6.		

What did you notice from this activity? Did things turn out better than you expected? This means the anxious thoughts did not have a strong connection with reality. Your anxious mind expects bad things to happen, but then they don't happen the way you expected. Reality testing is another way to calm your anxious mind.

thinking more calmly

for you to know

We can't stop difficult things from happening in our life. If you have an anxious mind, there's lots to worry about at school, home, and with your friends. This was Kendra's experience. As soon as she stepped outside the comfort and safety of her family, anxiety took over. Being around people she didn't know or traveling to unfamiliar places made her feel anxious.

You've learned a lot about your anxious mind from the activities you've done so far. Now it's time to put all that together and discover its opposite: your *calm mind*. With Kendra's experience as a guide, you can use your calm mind to counter the anxiety you feel from a distressing intrusive thought.

for you to do

1. Write down a situation, person, or experience that makes you feel anxious.

    My anxious concern: _____

    _____

    Kendra's example: Being around students and teachers I don't know.

2. Write down a distressing intrusive thought about your anxious concern:

    _____

    _____

    Kendra's example: What if a boy I don't know speaks to me and I freak out with anxiety?

3. Write a more calming way to think about the thing that makes you anxious. This will be your calm thinking story. Include the following points:

    a. Everyone has negative intrusive thoughts. Your calm thinking story includes ways the anxious thought is less threatening than you think.

    b. Remember the times you expected the worst, but it didn't happen. Write down what happened instead.

    c. State that your anxious thought is mainly connected to your imagination. Usually the anxious thinking has little connection with your daily life.

    d. Give examples of how you got on with your day despite having the anxious thought.

    e. Think about how you could turn the anxious intrusive thought into something positive. For example, your intrusive thinking could be a sign of creativity, a result of being a caring person, or part of a sensitive personality. Consider whether intrusive thinking helps you cope with problems in your life.

Kendra's calm thinking story: Probably most high school girls have thought they'd feel uncomfortable, maybe even awkward, talking to a boy they don't know. This has actually happened to me. I felt uncomfortable and awkward when a guy I didn't know spoke to me. But I never made a complete fool of myself. The anxious thought is my wild catastrophic imagination. The intrusive thought is a good reminder that I need to have more experience practicing my conversational skills. I can do this and accept that I'll be anxious at the same time.

My calm thinking story: _____

_____

_____

_____

_____

_____

_____

_____

_____

_____

You can use your calm thinking story whenever you have an anxious thought. It's a good way to switch off your anxious mind. When you do this, you'll feel less anxious. You may even feel calmer and more confident to handle difficult problems in your life.

more for you to do

Did you try writing a calm thinking story but it didn't help? You're still feeling anxious about the situation. Possibly you've felt anxious for so long that it's difficult to imagine the situation in a more calming way.

If this happened to you, imagine how a calm, non-anxious friend or family member might think about your anxious concern. For example, Kendra could write about how her calm and confident friend, Cassandra, thinks about the possibility of an unfamiliar boy speaking to her.

Write your non-anxious and confident friend's calm thinking story here. If you can't imagine this, ask your friend to help you with this exercise. Cassandra could tell Kendra what she thinks about when the thought of an unfamiliar boy speaking to her pops into her mind.

My friend's calm thinking story: _____

_____

_____

_____

_____

Now use ideas from your friend's calm thinking story to revise your calm thinking story.

My revised calm thinking story: _____

_____

_____

_____

_____

slay the dragon 17

for you to know

Are you afraid of your anxious thoughts? Do you try to escape from the anxious thought when it pops into your mind? Has it become a mental dragon that scares you? If this is happening to you, it's time to *slay the dragon*. This means facing the anxious thought and calmly staring it down.

There's a powerful strategy for conquering a fear of thoughts like this. Say you're worried about failing a math exam. Worry thoughts about the exam pop into your mind, and you keep trying to push them away. What if you set aside time and told yourself, *Every day for the next two weeks, I'll take thirty minutes and imagine the catastrophe of possibly failing the math exam*? Now you're taking control of the worry. At first, imagining the worst will make you feel more anxious, but the longer you think about the possibility of failing, the less anxious you're likely to feel. Soon you get bored with the activity. Maybe you also start thinking about ways to improve your exam preparation. You're switching from catastrophic thinking (*What if?*) to problem-solving thinking (*What can I do?*). Let's learn how to slay the worry dragon.

for you to do

Set aside thirty minutes each day to confront your anxious thoughts. Choose a location where you'll be comfortable and free from distractions. Have available the stories you developed with It's Not a Catastrophe (Activity 14) and Thinking More Calmly (Activity 16). And…go!

1. To get relaxed, take two to three minutes to focus on slow, deep breathing.

2. Bring to mind the anxious intrusive thought or worry. Focus all your attention on your catastrophic thinking. Remember how you think badly about yourself and exaggerate the possibility of something bad happening. It's important to make the experience as realistic as possible.

3. Read aloud your less extreme and calm thinking stories. Notice the reasons you realized that the anxious thought is a normal thought with only limited importance and threat. Keep reminding yourself that it's only a thought, and that something less threatening is more likely to happen. Allow five minutes for this step.

4. Return to focusing on your relaxing breathing for a couple of minutes.

5. Repeat steps 2 and 3 several times throughout the session.

6. Your mind will wander. Accept the distraction. Then gently bring your attention back to the anxious thought and your less extreme/calm thinking stories.

7. Use the following worksheet to write down your experience with this activity. (A downloadable version is available at http://www.newharbinger.com/48787.) Rate your anxiety at the beginning and at the end of the session on a 0 to 10 scale, where 0 = no anxiety, and 10 = intense, almost panicky anxiety.

Dragon Slayer Record Worksheet

Date	Session Length (in minutes)	Beginning Anxiety Rating (0–10)	Ending Anxiety Rating (0–10)

As you repeat this activity, you'll find that:

- The more you slay the worry dragon, the less you'll fear your anxious intrusive thoughts.

- You'll become better able to shift from an anxious mind to a calmer way of thinking.

After doing several "dragon slayer" sessions, did you feel less anxious?

more for you to do

If your anxiety doesn't lessen after repeated sessions, try making these changes:

- The anxious thought you're working on may be too intense. Start with a less anxious thought, gradually working your way up to more anxious ones.

- Notice if you're getting stuck on stinking thinking and catastrophizing. Make sure you're shifting your thinking to the less extreme and calm thinking stories.

- Be patient! It's hard to predict how many sessions you'll need to start feeling less anxious.

- If you start feeling more depressed, discouraged, or hopeless, stop doing the activity and concentrate on some of the other activities in the workbook. It is not helpful to continue an activity that makes you feel worse, not better.

PART 4

Let Go of Control

18 overthinking

for you to know

Do you spend a lot of time in your head? Are you a deep thinker? If you are, congratulations! Being a deep thinker is a great quality. It's linked to success in school, relationships, and self-awareness.

It's important to pay attention to your thoughts and to understand what they mean. But it's easy to overdo deep thinking. When thoughts pop into your mind, do you get caught up in searching for their cause or what might happen because you're having the thought? If this describes you, then you may be *overthinking*.

Overthinking starts with searching your mind for unwanted thoughts, images, or memories. You find an anxious thought, then spend too much time trying to understand its meaning. You struggle to get control over your mind and end up "stuck in your head," your mind filling with sticky anxious thoughts.

Overthinkers are more likely to feel anxious from their unwanted thoughts than people who don't overthink. Are you wondering if you're an overthinker? The next exercise lists some characteristics of overthinking.

for you to do

Read each statement and check the ones that describe you.

- ☐ *It's easy to tune in to what I'm thinking at any moment.*

- ☐ *I understand how my mind works.*

- ☐ *I often question or second-guess what I'm thinking.*

- ☐ *I often try to change the way I think about things in my life.*

- ☐ *I often become upset by unwanted thoughts that pop into my mind.*

- ☐ *I am easily distracted by my thinking.*

- ☐ *I often ask myself,* What am I thinking at this moment?

- ☐ *It's important that I have control over unwanted thoughts that pop into my mind.*

- ☐ *I'm a thoughtful, self-aware person.*

- ☐ *I'm a deep thinker.*

- ☐ *I'm detail-oriented, so it's hard to let go of problems.*

- ☐ *I often look for the deeper meaning in everything.*

- ☐ *I have a strong need to know, to understand.*

- ☐ *I have a hard time handling uncertainty or situations that are vague or confusing.*

If you checked seven or more statements, overthinking may be an important reason for your anxious feelings. Do small things like an unexpected text message from a friend, a hasty comment, or a rude remark trigger an endless cycle of mental analysis? Once overthinking kicks into gear, it can be hard to do anything else. It can feel like your mind is racing out of control. And when this happens, the anxiety and worry build along with it.

more for you to do

If you've realized overthinking is a problem for you, it's important to break the habit. It starts by knowing when you're overthinking and telling yourself to stop it. Here's how to practice "calling yourself out" on overthinking:

1. Review the anxious intrusive thoughts you recorded in previous activities.

2. Ask yourself, *Do I overanalyze these thoughts when they pop into my head?*

3. Create a phrase you can use when you catch overthinking; for example: *There I go again! I'm getting sucked into overthinking. I'm just going in circles, chasing my tail. It's only making me more frustrated and upset.*

4. Write a statement that encourages you to stop overthinking; for example: *Overthinking again! It's best to stop analyzing my anxious thoughts. There's probably no deep meaning to discover. Besides, how would I know whether I've found the right meaning? Just accept the anxious thought for what it is—an anxious thought—and leave it at that.*

   Your statement to stop overthinking: _____

   _____

   _____

   _____

Once you've written out your *stop overthinking statement*, practice catching yourself overthinking. Repeat the statement to yourself and concentrate on its meaning. Do this again and again each time you overthink. Notice whether over time you're doing less overthinking.

the mental control myth 19

for you to know

Remember the white bear experiment (Activity 6)? Trying to not think about something is very difficult. And then there was the work you did in Trying Hard to Not Think (Activity 10). The harder you try to not think about something, the more you think about it. That's the *mental control paradox*: We simply can't control unwanted thoughts. So why do we keep trying to do it?

The answer lies in the *mental control myth*. When we're anxious, we think the answer is to try harder to mentally control our thoughts and feeling. It goes like this:

My anxious thoughts are out of control because I'm not trying hard enough to control them. If I try harder to push the thought from my mind, my anxiety will go away.

Have you fallen for the mental control myth? If so, you know it just makes your anxiety worse. You try harder to not think anxiously. But then the mental control paradox kicks in. Now you're having more anxious thoughts, not fewer.

for you to do

The mental control myth says we'll feel better if we have more control. Let's test this with a mood/mental control investigation. Over the next week, record your mood changes using the following worksheet. (A downloadable version is available at http://www.newharbinger.com/48787.)

Note your positive moods: happy, excited, interested, calm. Then rate the intensity of the feeling on a three-point scale (1 = mild, 2 = moderate, 3 = strong).

Note your negative moods: sad, fearful, anxious, frustrated, irritated, guilty. Rate the intensity on the three-point scale (1 = mild, 2 = moderate, 3 = strong).

Each time you record a positive or negative feeling, rate how much mental control effort you put into making yourself have that feeling. Rate your mental control effort on a four-point scale (0 = no effort, 1 = slight effort, 2 = moderate effort, 3 = strong effort).

Mood and Control Worksheet

Positive Mood	Intensity of Mood State	Mental Control Effort	Negative Mood	Intensity of Mood State	Mental Control Effort

This activity is about testing whether you feel the way you do because of your thought control efforts. For example, if you felt happy, was that because you were trying to have happy thoughts? If you felt only mildly anxious, was that because you tried hard to push anxious thoughts or worry from your mind?

more for you to do

Take a moment to answer the following questions:

1. What did you notice about changes in your mood and efforts to control your thoughts? Did you feel best only when you tried hard to have positive thoughts? Was your mood worse only when you had low control over your negative thoughts?

    _____

    _____

2. How often did you have a good mood without any effort to control your thoughts?

    _____

    _____

3. How often were you in a bad mood even though you tried hard to change your thinking?

    _____

    _____

This activity is a myth buster. There are many things that affect our mood. Trying harder to control your thoughts has less influence on how you feel than you think. You've learned some strategies to deal with your anxious thoughts. Greater mental control effort is not one of them.

for you to know

Do you like psychological thrillers? One theme often seen in these movies is the idea of *snapping*. It goes like this: The main character is a calm, very normal person. Something happens, and suddenly the person "snaps" and does something we consider irrational. They may start acting very strange—or turn into a cold-blooded killer.

This idea of losing control of your mind and doing something irrational, something you would later regret, is a common fear. You're probably not afraid of turning into a killer or completely losing touch with reality. But you might fear having a panic attack, crying uncontrollably, or losing your temper. These emotional states all involve feeling you've lost all control.

The fear of snapping is another reason why people think they need to keep strict control over their mind. They think *My mind is fragile, so I need to be careful what I think. If I don't, something bad could happen, like a complete emotional breakdown.* This fear of losing mental control is another reason we can struggle with intrusive thoughts. But what if your anxiety is caused by *too much* mental control, not too little? Decreasing your fear of losing control of your thoughts could actually help reduce anxiety and worry. You would become more accepting and more at peace with your thoughts and feelings, even the ones you don't want.

for you to do

Is complete loss of mental control a reasonable fear? We all have limited control over our thoughts and feelings—that's not the issue. Snapping means *completely* losing control. We fear this happening, leading to an emotional meltdown. But what is your actual risk of snapping?

Write down up to five times when you had an emotional meltdown—seriously losing control over your thoughts, feelings, or behavior. Maybe this negatively affected you or others. Maybe you felt embarrassed or upset.

1. _____

2. _____

3. _____

4. _____

5. _____

Think about these experiences and decide whether you *snapped completely* or were just afraid you might. Now write beside each experience either "snapped" or "feared snapping."

Which happened the most—actually losing control or fearing you would? For most people, the fear is more common. It's important to know that we usually have more control than we think, even during times of intense emotion.

more for you to do

Are intrusive thoughts dangerous if we don't control them? Could they cause us to snap? To answer these questions, review the emotional experiences you just listed and write your responses.

1. Did you *actually* lose complete control, or did you *feel* like you were losing control?

   _____

2. Did you show poor self-control or absolutely no self-control ("losing it")?

   _____

   _____

3. Is there evidence you had some control?

   _____

   _____

4. Was the emotional experience caused by intrusive thoughts? Could you have prevented the experience by having greater control over your thoughts?

   _____

   _____

What do your answers tell you? Did you bust the snapping myth? It's possible you had poor self-control and ended up hurting yourself or others with your rage. If this is true, then I encourage you to seek help with your emotions. But you don't have to fear your intrusive thoughts. And overcontrolling your thoughts is not the answer to fear of losing control. A better way to reduce anxiety is to not try so hard to control anxious intrusive thoughts. Exaggerating your loss of control over anxious thoughts will only make them more frightening.

21 the wrong way

for you to know

It's hard to get to where you want to go if you're going the wrong way. And it's hard to get control over your anxious thoughts if you use the wrong strategy. You've learned that trying too hard to control your thoughts is not effective. But when we're anxious, it's hard to do nothing. So consider what you do when you have unwanted thoughts and feelings—it will determine whether you continue to struggle or find relief.

Imagine that it's your last year of high school and you don't know what to do next year. Should you apply to university, take a year off to travel, or work? The thought *What should I do?* pops into your mind constantly, making you anxious. You don't simply ignore the thought; you try to control it by thinking of something else or pushing it out of your mind. But some thought control methods are not so effective when you're anxious. We'll call these *weak mental control strategies*. If you're using these strategies to deal with anxious thoughts, you'll benefit from recognizing this—and replacing them with the helpful ones you'll learn in this workbook.

for you to do

This table lists five weak mental control strategies. Place a checkmark beside the strategies you tend to use when trying to control anxious thoughts and feelings. (Tip: You might find it helpful to review your ratings on the Mental Control Strategies in Activity 10.)

Control Strategy	Definition	Example
☐ Unfocused distraction	Jumping from one distracting thought or activity to another.	Thinking about your friends, then about schoolwork, then about sports, and so on.
☐ Self-criticism	Criticizing yourself for being anxious.	Calling yourself names like weak, stupid, or loser.
☐ Compulsion	Doing or thinking something repeatedly to get rid of an anxious thought.	Repeating a calming phrase like *calm blue ocean*.
☐ Reassurance seeking	Asking other people or searching on the internet for information that you hope will make you feel better.	Insisting that your parents reassure you that you'll pass your math final.
☐ Rationalization	Trying to convince yourself that everything will be fine.	You're going out with someone for the first time, and trying to convince yourself that everything will be fine; he won't be able to tell you're nervous. You'll be interesting and funny, so he'll want to see you again.

Which of these strategies do you use most? Some, like unfocused distraction and reassurance seeking, are more common than others. And some strategies, like self-criticism and compulsions, are more harmful. But not a single one is very helpful in gaining control over your anxious thinking. You'll discover more effective mental control strategies in later activities. For now, be aware that anxious thoughts may be sticking in your mind because you're using weak mental control methods.

more for you to do

Maybe you had difficulty using the table because you're not sure whether you use these weak control strategies. Most of us don't pay attention to how we try to control our anxious thoughts. We're more focused on the thought itself and how we feel.

If in doubt, go back and review the anxious thoughts you entered in your Anxious Intrusions Diary (Activity 8). Read each entry and write in the margin whether your response to an anxious thought included one of the weak mental control strategies. If you have only one or two entries in your diary, use the diary to keep track of your anxious thinking for the next two weeks. Note times when you used a weak mental control strategy.

Are you surprised to learn that you're using weak mental control methods when you have anxious thoughts? This could be another reason for having sticky anxious thoughts. Don't be discouraged. We'll show you better ways to deal with the stinking thinking that's making you feel anxious and worried.

when distraction fails 22

for you to know

Let's say you have an anxious thought like *My parents are going to be so angry at me.* You know there's going to be a big blowup when you get home. But right now you're with your friends. You want to have a good time. You don't want to be all stressed out with anxiety and worry. So you want to stop thinking about your parents. You try to think of something else, anything but your parents! What you're doing is called *distraction*— the most common method we use to control our thoughts. Distraction is such an automatic response to unwanted thoughts that its very presence makes it hard for us to let go of trying to control our anxious thinking.

There are different types of distraction. Some are more effective than others. The problem is, we naturally rely on less effective distraction, which makes us think more about an unwanted anxious thought rather than less.

Distraction becomes ineffective when you keep jumping from topic to topic. For example, you don't want to think about your parents being angry at you. So you try to think of something else, like a text message you just got from a friend. You think about the text, but then your parents pop back into your mind. You try to think about your history assignment, but soon your parents return. You think about last night's basketball game, but it doesn't stick; the parent thought returns. Now you've been thinking of a bunch of other things along with the parent thought. This means you now have many different thoughts that remind you of the angry parent thought! It's much better to use one distracting thought than a bunch of different ones.

for you to do

Did you ever wonder why distraction only works sometimes? Try this activity. Over the next week, select Tuesday, Thursday, and Saturday as high mental control days and Monday, Wednesday, Friday, and Sunday as low mental control days.

During low-control days, let your anxious thoughts come and go without trying to push them from your mind. When you have an anxious thought, let it sit in your mind and get on with whatever you're doing at that moment. Act as if you're not having the thought, even though it's present in your mind.

On high-control days, pay close attention to your anxious thoughts. Try hard to not think about the anxious thought by distracting yourself with many different thoughts or activities.

In the worksheet, summarize your experience with high versus low mental control. (A downloadable version is available at http://www.newharbinger.com/48787.) Did you feel anxious? How severe was it? How long did it last? What happened to the anxious thought when you tried to control it? What happened to the thought when you *didn't* try to control it?

Control Effort Worksheet

Days	High Mental Control Effort (Using lots of distractions to force yourself to not think an anxious thought)	Low Mental Control Effort (Letting the anxious thought drift naturally through your mind)
Monday		
Tuesday		
Wednesday		
Thursday		
Friday		
Saturday		
Sunday		

Now explore what you've discovered. Was your anxiety better or worse on high-control or low-control days?

more for you to do

Answer the following questions to better understand how distraction might make it more difficult to let go of control over anxious thoughts:

1. Did you have more anxious thoughts and more distress on high-control days versus low-control days? Or was there no difference?

   _____

2. Were you more frustrated or stressed out on high-control days when you were using lots of distractions?

   _____

3. Is there any reason to continue trying to distract yourself from anxious thoughts? If distraction doesn't work, why do it?

   _____

   _____

   _____

   _____

You likely discovered that your anxiety is no better when you're trying hard to control anxious thoughts. The activities in part 5 will show you better ways to handle your anxious thoughts and feelings.

Self-Acceptance

23 practice self-acceptance

for you to know

Does it sometimes feel like you're losing the battle against anxiety? This happens when you give anxious thoughts more importance than they deserve, and when you try too hard to control them. Since it's impossible to stop your brain from having negative and anxious thoughts, what can you do? You can practice greater self-acceptance of your negative thoughts and feelings.

Self-acceptance is the ability to accept what's not going well in your life without feeling defeated. It's a willingness to allow your mind to experience negative thoughts and feelings. People with low self-acceptance often don't like themselves. They fight against their mind, trying to change it by pushing out negative thoughts and feelings. They might say to themselves, *I've got to stop thinking so negatively and be more positive.*

People with high self-acceptance have a higher level of self-liking. They realize that sometimes they'll have negative and anxious thoughts. They're able to think *All my thoughts can't be positive. It's okay to have a negative or anxious thought pop into my mind. I'll just let the thought sit there and get on with my day.*

Are there things you don't like about yourself? If so, you'll benefit from boosting your self-acceptance to feel less anxious. It's hard to change your approach to anxious thoughts if you struggle to accept who you are.

for you to do

Read the example in the following worksheet. (A downloadable version is available at http://www.newharbinger.com/48787.) Then think back to five of your most difficult experiences. For each, describe how you dealt with the problem. Were you able to consider the thoughts an unpleasant experience rather than a catastrophe?

Self-Acceptance Worksheet

Difficult Experience	Were You Self-Critical or Understanding Toward Yourself?	Did You Try to Change Your Thinking or Just Let Anxious Thoughts Sit in Your Mind?
I discovered my boyfriend was cheating on me with my best friend. I needed to confront him but was scared to do it.	At first I blamed myself, thinking I was not as good as my friend. But then I was more understanding toward myself, realizing that cheating reflected their poor characters, not mine.	I kept telling myself to forget about it, but I couldn't. I realized I wouldn't stop thinking about it until I confronted him.
1.		
2.		

Difficult Experience	Were You Self-Critical or Understanding Toward Yourself?	Did You Try to Change Your Thinking or Just Let Anxious Thoughts Sit in Your Mind?
3.		
4.		
5.		

Review the experiences you've described. Difficulties in life test our level of self-acceptance. Were you able to be more understanding of yourself? Did you allow yourself to experience negative thoughts and feelings? If you tried to control the negative thoughts by pushing them out of your mind, you were expressing low self-acceptance.

more for you to do

Review each of the difficult experiences you recorded in the Self-Acceptance
Worksheet. In the space provided, describe how you could have shown more kindness
and consideration toward yourself. No doubt you know how to be kind to other
people. Being kind to yourself may be less familiar. Essentially, self-kindness is
showing compassion toward yourself when you make a mistake or fail to meet your
expectations. It's the opposite of being harsh, critical, and judgmental. Instead of
criticizing yourself for having negative or anxious thoughts, you accept that unwanted
thoughts will pop into your mind from time to time.

1. _____

_____

2. _____

_____

3. _____

_____

4. _____

_____

5. _____

_____

Is self-acceptance a new idea for you? If so, you likely found this activity challenging.
Ask a parent, another adult who's a close friend, or your therapist for help with
the activity. Developing a kinder, gentler, more patient attitude toward yourself is
important. You'll be more successful in developing a calm mind when you are more
self-accepting.

24 mind wandering

for you to know

We've been talking about intrusive thoughts that suddenly pop into your mind. Often these thoughts are anxious and lead to anxious feelings. You've also been learning that much of our thinking is not under our control. We daydream, our mind wanders in different directions, and we have intrusive thoughts. People with high self-acceptance are fine with this spontaneous thinking. But if you have an anxious mind and your self-acceptance is low, all this spontaneous thinking can be upsetting. Spontaneous thinking is often difficult for overthinkers. They can easily get caught up in trying to figure out what the thoughts mean.

Are you a natural daydreamer? Can you let go of control and allow yourself to freely enjoy any thought that pops into your mind? This can be difficult when you have an anxious mind. Anxious thoughts and worry can creep in at any moment, so you may believe you need to be on the lookout for anxious thoughts to keep tight control over your mind. It can feel strange and wrong to "take your foot off the brake" and let your mind wander freely.

Yet by practicing letting your mind wander freely, you can develop greater self-acceptance. With a wandering mind, you're taking a chance that any thought, even an anxious one, might pop into it. Mind wandering requires a more accepting, open attitude toward your thoughts. This next activity lets you practice more acceptance and comfort with your wandering mind.

for you to do

Practice taking a five-minute break several times a day to let your mind wander. This should be done in your free time, not when you're supposed to pay attention, like in school or other times when you're receiving instruction. Think of it as a mini relaxation or meditation break.

Begin each break with a few relaxing breaths. Then simply let your mind wander. Allow yourself to think about whatever pops into your mind. Don't control what you think, force yourself to have certain thoughts, or try to stop any thoughts from entering your mind. Just let yourself daydream throughout the five-minute break.

At the end of day, use the Mind Wandering Record to summarize your experience with mind wandering breaks. (A downloadable version is available at http://www .newharbinger.com/48787.) Then use a ten-point scale to rate how well you tolerated or were comfortable with mind wandering, with 0 = no tolerance of spontaneous thoughts, and 10 = completely tolerant of anything that popped into your mind.

Mind Wandering Record

Day	My Mind Wandering Experiences	Rating of Tolerance/ Comfort
Sunday		
Monday		
Tuesday		
Wednesday		
Thursday		
Friday		
Saturday		

At the end of the first week, review your Mind Wandering Record. With practice, did you become more comfortable with letting your mind wander?

more for you to do

To gain more from this exercise, take a moment to explore your experience.

1. List any anxious thoughts that popped into your mind during your mind-wandering breaks:

   _____   _____

   _____   _____

   _____   _____

2. If you had anxious thoughts, how well did you accept or tolerate them?

   _____

3. Was there anything about the anxious thoughts that made them intolerable or difficult to accept?

   _____

4. List any positive or pleasant thoughts that popped into your mind during mind wandering:

   _____   _____

   _____   _____

   _____   _____

Mind wandering is a good way to develop more acceptance of your thoughts and feelings. If you felt uncomfortable with mind wandering, it's a good activity to keep practicing. If you found the activity super easy, feel free to move on to the next—a different way to develop greater acceptance of your wandering mind.

25 mindful acceptance

for you to know

Are you familiar with mindfulness? It's the experience of paying attention to your thoughts and feelings in the present moment without being critical. In practicing *mindful acceptance*, we observe all our thoughts and feelings, even the negative ones, in an open, gentle, and kind manner. There's no attempt to control or criticize yourself for having anxious thoughts or feelings. You might say to yourself, *Oh, there's that anxious thought again. Hello, anxious thought. You weren't gone long. Are you going to stay in my mind for a while?* Notice you don't get taken in by the thought. You treat it as an uninvited guest in your mind.

Imagine that you struggle with anxiety and worry about doing well in school. Let's say you frequently have the anxious thought *I'll never do well on this test, exam, or assignment.* An anxious mind would immediately react to this thought. It might be critical, saying *Don't be so negative or hard on yourself.* It might try to control the thought, believing that thinking this way could lead you to get a poor mark.

A mindful acceptance approach would recognize the anxious thought. It wouldn't judge or try to control the thought. It would observe it, treating it as a thought, not a fact. In mindful acceptance you wrap the anxious thought in kindness, love, and patience. At first this might sound like an unusual approach to anxious thinking, but with practice you'll feel more and more comfortable with this kinder, gentler approach to your anxiety.

for you to do

You can practice mindful acceptance throughout the day. Whenever you have an anxious thought, follow these steps:

1. Stop what you're doing. Focus your attention on what you're thinking at that moment. Ask yourself, *What am I thinking and feeling right now?*

2. Imagine your anxious thought is a person. You open your arms and hug the anxious thought. This may sound weird, but give it a chance. You're using your imagination to experience anxious thoughts in a kind, open, loving manner. You're creating a visual image of full acceptance of the anxious thought.

3. Hold on to this accepting image for five minutes or so. If you now feel less anxious about the intrusive thought, return to what you were doing. If you're still anxious, repeat the first two steps.

You can evaluate your mindful acceptance experiences using the Mindful Acceptance Record. (A downloadable version is available at http://www.newharbinger.com/48787.) Make a daily rating of how often you practiced mindful acceptance. Use a ten-point scale, where 0 = not at all (did not practice mindfulness today), and 10 = you always practiced mindful acceptance whenever you had an anxious thought. Next, rate your self-acceptance or ability to tolerate the anxious thoughts: 0 = you experienced no self-acceptance (could not tolerate the anxious thought), and 10 = you experienced complete self-acceptance (were able to embrace the anxious thought).

Mindful Acceptance Record

Day	Mindful Practice (0–10 scale)	Self-Acceptance/ Tolerance (0–10 scale)
Sunday		
Monday		
Tuesday		
Wednesday		
Thursday		
Friday		
Saturday		

After spending two weeks practicing mindful acceptance, review your Mindful Acceptance Record. Is your acceptance or tolerance of anxious thoughts improving with practice?

more for you to do

If you haven't found mindful acceptance helpful with your anxiety, check the statements in this troubleshooting checklist that apply to you:

☐ *Most of the time when I had anxious thoughts I didn't even try using mindful acceptance.*

☐ *I had a hard time simply observing my anxious thoughts and worries; instead, I got completely absorbed by them.*

☐ *I'm not good at visualizing things, especially something like "hugging" my anxious thoughts.*

☐ *It's hard to believe mindful acceptance could help reduce my anxious feelings.*

☐ *It's hard for me to express love and kindness to anyone, especially myself.*

Any of these can get in the way of your benefiting from mindful acceptance. Consider what changes you could make so that mindful acceptance has a more positive influence on your anxious thinking.

PART 6

Build on Your Strengths

26 make distraction work

for you to know

Imagine you see a posting on social media from your best friend. She's kissing up to one of the popular girls who has said mean things about you in the past. You feel betrayed. How could she do this to you? Every time you think about it, you feel so upset. Yet if you say anything you'll seem jealous and pathetic. How can you stop thinking about it and get on with your life?

A great way to stop unwanted thoughts is with *focused distraction*. Don't get me wrong—this is no ordinary distraction. Focused distraction is special. It involves directing your attention to a *single highly interesting idea, memory, or activity*. When you want to stop thinking about something, like your best friend and the mean classmate, you might try to distract yourself, but your mind just jumps around, and everything reminds you of the betrayal. We call this *unfocused distraction*, and it's not effective (see Activity 22 for more strategies).

With focused distraction, you think about only one thing. Let's say you've been trying out for the cheerleadering team. The competition is pretty grueling, so very few make the cut. So whenever the thought of your friend's betrayal pops into your mind, you decide you will immediately start thinking about the cheerleading tryouts. You focus your mind on cheerleading for several minutes, thinking about every detail of the competition. A good focused distraction will be very interesting to you and might lead to a positive outcome. A very interesting distraction will divert your attention from the anxious thought, and a positive one is more likely to put you in a good mood.

for you to do

This next activity is essential for making focused distraction work for you. You'll use the following Distraction List to record your most interesting memories, activities, and daydreams. (A downloadable version is available at http://www.newharbinger. com/48787.) Do this activity when you're in a good mood and have time to think about your positive, interesting past experiences and activities. First list at least five positive memories that involve success, happiness, or enjoyment. Next, list several activities that make you happy, like playing sports, music, or just hanging out with friends. In the third column, write down some of your daydreams or how you imagine your future in a positive way.

You can enter your distraction list into your phone. The next time you have an anxious thought, select a distraction and spend time thinking about it. Did your attention shift from the anxious thought to the distraction? Did you then feel less anxious?

Distraction List

Memories	Activities	Daydreams
1.		
2.		
3.		
4.		
5.		

more for you to do

If you're not sure you've listed effective distractions, try them out. When you're in a good mood, spend ten to fifteen minutes thinking deeply about each distraction. From the following list, check each statement that accurately describes your experience with the distraction.

☐ *I was thinking about something very important to me—not something minor or trivial in my life.*

☐ *What I was thinking about is fairly complicated, with a lot of detail that required my concentration.*

☐ *When I was thinking about the memory, activity, or daydream, I felt pretty good. What I was thinking about is very positive, so I really enjoyed paying attention to it.*

☐ *When I was thinking about the distraction, I actually lost track of time. I really got into it.*

☐ *When I'm bored or trying to get to sleep, the distraction is one of the things that I think about.*

If most of your distractions meet these five characteristics, then you have a good list of effective distractions. If you're still unsure, ask a close friend, parent, or other family member what they see as your greatest interests or passions, then add these to your distraction list.

27 take action with distraction

for you to know

With your distraction list in hand, it's now time to put it into action. When you start to think anxiously, replace those thoughts with a topic from your distraction list. Maybe you've tried to distract yourself before and it hasn't helped. But remember, focused distraction is different from ordinary distraction. In focused distraction we follow specific steps to find the most effective distraction rather than trying to distract ourselves with the first thing that pops into our mind.

for you to do

The following diagram illustrates the steps in focused distraction. It starts with an unwanted anxious thought that pops into your mind. Next, you recognize you're having the anxious thought and remember why it's less important than you think. (If you can't remember why your anxious thoughts are not so important, review the work you did in Activities 9 and 12.)

The critical step in focused distraction is thinking deeply about a distraction that you've chosen from your list. As you are thinking of every detail about the distraction, you focus on breathing calmly. Take slow, deep breaths so you're feeling a little more relaxed as you think about the distraction. After ten minutes or so in distracting thought, end with becoming involved in a distracting activity like updating your social media profile, tidying up your room, or doing a homework assignment. You can use focused distraction any time an anxious thought pops into your mind, as long as it doesn't interfere with a current activity.

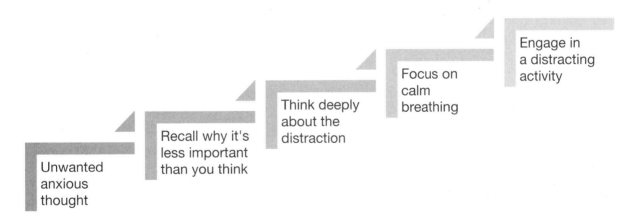

Remember these points about using focused distraction to deal with anxious thinking:

* *Practice, practice, practice.* Focused distraction may look simple, but it's harder than you think. Keep practicing with a variety of distractions. You're learning a thought control skill, so it'll take time.

- *Challenge its importance.* Focused distraction works only if you realize the anxious thought is not so important. Review the activities you did in part 3 to remind yourself that what you're anxious about is not a catastrophe.

- *Think deeply.* When turning your attention to the distraction, you'll need to remember lots of detail, so it has your full concentration. You want your mind absorbed in the distraction.

- *Breathe.* As you are thinking, you can switch your focus from the distraction to your breathing, taking slow, deep breaths. It's easier to concentrate on the distraction when you feel more relaxed.

- *Expect mental intrusions.* The anxious thought and other intrusive thoughts will pop into your mind. Simply welcome the intrusion, sit with it for a couple of seconds, and then gently return your attention to the distraction.

- *End with an activity.* It's not good to sit for long periods doing mental control exercises. Instead, move on to a chore or activity that moves your body.

more for you to do

It's easy to slip back into unfocused distraction. To improve your mental retraining efforts, keep a log of your focused distraction experiences. (A downloadable version is available at http://www.newharbinger.com/48787.) It'll help you keep on track and focused on being focused. At bedtime, take a few minutes to fill in the day's activity sheet. It's a simple count of how often you used focused distraction and whether it was effective in reducing anxious thinking.

Rate its effectiveness using a scale of 0 = not effective, 1 = slightly effective, 2 = moderately effective, 3 = fairly effective, 4 = very effective.

Focused Distraction Log

Date	Number of Times You Used Focused Distraction	Effectiveness in Reducing Anxious Thinking

After your first week of doing focused distraction, review your log. If you tried focused distraction only a couple of times, you're not practicing enough to become skillful, especially if you had frequent anxious thoughts during the week. This means you are missing opportunities to practice focused distraction. If your effectiveness ratings were also low, your distractions may be too trivial, so it's hard for you to think deeply about them. Also, distractions should be about positive things in your life. Focused distraction is a mental control skill; like any skill, it requires training and practice to master.

28 do it later

for you to know

"I'll do it later!" How often have you heard yourself say this when your parents want you to do a chore? You're doing something really interesting, and you don't want to stop to clean your room, do dishes, or mow the lawn. So you say the first thing that pops into your mind: "I'll do it later." It's so easy to say. But then you forget to do the chore. And now your parents are really upset.

Have you ever thought about how easy it is to put off doing something that is unpleasant or boring or you just don't want to do? What if you used the same approach to your unwanted anxious and distressing thoughts? What if you treated the anxious thought as if it were your parent asking you to do something unpleasant? We call this *postponement*, and it's a really simple strategy for dealing with anxious thoughts and worry. You're already used to saying "I'll do it later"—why not put your procrastination skill to good use when you have an anxious thought or worry?

for you to do

Here's how to make thought postponement work for you:

1. **Label the thought.** When the anxious thought pops into your mind, say to yourself, *An anxious thought about _____ just popped into my mind.*

2. **Accept the thought.** Remind yourself that the anxious thought is unwanted, that you're not trying to think this way, and that it's just one of the hundreds of thoughts that pop into your mind.

3. **Record the thought.** Jot down any new information or discovery that has come to you about what makes you feel anxious.

4. **Delay the thought.** Instead of spending time on the thought now, promise yourself that later that day you'll set aside thirty minutes or so to think more deeply about the thing that's making you anxious. Use the "slay the dragon" technique described in Activity 17.

Anxious thoughts can pop into your mind many times during the day. Whenever they do, repeat these steps. The more you do this, the more effective it can be.

more for you to do

So you've told yourself to *think about it later*, but you can't get the anxious thought out of your mind. There are several possible reasons why. Review the following troubleshooting statements and check any that apply to the anxious thought you're trying to postpone. The suggested activities will help you make postponement more effective.

☐ *The anxious thought still feels like a real personal threat* (Activities 9 and 12).

☐ *I quickly slip into catastrophic thinking when the thought pops into my mind* (Activity 14).

☐ *It's almost impossible to imagine anything but the worst possible outcome* (Activity 16).

☐ *I can't seem to reality test the anxious thought. I get caught up imagining what* could *happen rather than what is most likely to happen* (Activity 15).

☐ *I try too hard to push the anxious thought from my mind* (Activity 10).

☐ *I'm too harsh and self-critical for letting the thought back into my mind* (Activity 23).

☐ *I'm overthinking the anxious thought* (Activity 18).

If you checked any statements, you may need to spend more time on the recommended activities to reduce the emotional intensity of the anxious thought. Once you do that, you'll be able to say *I'll think about it later.*

recognize your goodness 29

for you to know

It's natural to get down on yourself when you feel anxious and worried. Anxiety makes us feel weak, insecure, and worthless. It's easy to get stuck on what's going wrong in your life and then start blaming yourself. When this happens, we become negative and self-critical. We tend to overlook our strengths and good qualities. This negativity can sap our emotional strength and make it much harder to deal with anxious thoughts and feelings.

Psychologists have found that taking time to think about your positive qualities can improve how you feel about yourself and even help you gain better control over unwanted distressing thoughts. This practice of *self-affirmation* is another good way to deal with anxious thoughts and worry.

for you to do

Most of us don't spend time thinking about what's good about ourselves. We might have a random positive thought from time to time, but that's about it. For self-affirmation to stop anxious thinking, you need to deliberately discover your positive qualities. Then you can use positive thoughts to counter your anxious thinking. You'll also feel better about yourself because you're now recognizing your strengths and positive characteristics.

First, spend some time thinking about who you are in different areas of your life. The following worksheet lists several important areas of living—school, family, friends, and so on. (A downloadable version is available at http://www.newharbinger .com/48787.) In each area that is relevant for you, write down two qualities that help you succeed or be a good person. For example, under school, you might list *hardworking, responsible,* or *intelligent.* For friends, you might list *reliable, understanding,* or *loyal.* In the second column, write down some specific examples of how you show this good quality in each area of your life. For school, you might list as an example of hard work and intelligence *Studied hard for the history midterm and got a better mark than I expected.*

Positive Qualities Worksheet

Positive Qualities	Examples of How You Showed Your Positive Quality
School: 1. 2.	
Family: 1. 2.	

Friends: 1. 2.	
Physical Fitness: 1. 2.	
Recreation/Sports/Music: 1. 2.	
Community/Volunteer: 1. 2.	
Faith/Spiritual/Moral: 1. 2.	

Review your completed table and circle your strongest good qualities. When an anxious thought pops into your mind, remind yourself of one of these good qualities and your related examples. You're replacing the anxious thought with a positive thought about one of your good qualities.

more for you to do

Was this activity too difficult? Maybe you're not used to thinking of yourself as having good qualities. You could ask a parent, family member, or close friend for suggestions of what they think are your good qualities. (You'll also find some examples of positive qualities listed in the free tools at http://www.newharbinger.com/48787.) Choose any of these qualities that you recognize as applying to you.

You can also strengthen self-affirmation by writing down times when you succeeded at something, did something good for others, acted responsibly, followed your moral values or conscience, or expressed your goodness in other ways. Several times a week, review what you've written and think about these experiences as examples of your good qualities.

PART 7

Boost Happiness

30 how positive are you?

for you to know

Are there times when you feel good and you don't know why? Strong feelings of joy, peace, or excitement hit you out of the blue. It's not due to some great news, but you just feel so good. When this happens, it's likely you're having *positive intrusive thoughts*. Spontaneous positive thoughts and feelings are a good remedy for anxious thinking. But positive feelings don't last long. They evaporate like the morning dew on a hot summer day. Training yourself to pay more attention to your positive intrusive thoughts is another great way to reduce anxiety in your life.

We all have different natural tendencies when it comes to positive thoughts and happiness. Do you have friends who seem happy much of the time? They're always laughing, telling funny stories, and being quite positive about most things. Maybe you have another friend who is down much of the time, very serious, and tends to be quite negative. And the rest of your friends are somewhere on the spectrum in between.

Everyone has a different starting point for happiness. It's important to discover your own natural level of positive thoughts and feelings. It's probably unrealistic to think you could become a super positive person who's happy all the time. Trying to reach an impossible goal is discouraging and will only cause you to give up. But you can aim to improve your experience of positive thoughts and feelings. And you can work on being more aware of your spontaneous positive thoughts so they have a bigger impact on your life.

for you to do

Let's begin with a self-discovery activity. Read these statements about life experiences and check the ones that describe you:

☐ *Generally I feel satisfied with my life.*

☐ *I often feel joy, peace, pride, or fun.*

☐ *I'm quite optimistic about my future.*

☐ *I rarely worry about the future.*

☐ *I rarely feel guilty, sad, anxious, or frustrated.*

☐ *I have life goals and ambitions.*

☐ *Most of the time I feel like I'm in control of my life.*

☐ *I have close and loving relationships.*

☐ *My life is full of meaning and purpose.*

☐ *I think I'm a good person with as much worth and value as others.*

If you checked most of the statements, it's likely you're a fairly positive person. No doubt you experience frequent positive intrusive thoughts about yourself and your life circumstances. If you checked only one or two statements, you likely have a natural tendency to be more negative. You have the potential to improve your positivity by paying more attention to the occasional positive intrusive thoughts that pop into your mind.

Now that you know your starting point for being positive, Activity 31 will help you raise your positivity by paying more attention to spontaneous positive thoughts.

more for you to do

It's really hard to be honest with ourselves. The checklist statements refer to very positive characteristics. Did you find it hard to admit that you aren't presently a happy, optimistic, and enthusiastic person? Or do you tend to be too hard on yourself? Maybe some of these statements do describe you, but you don't see it. Why not ask a parent, close family member, or good friend that you trust to complete the checklist for you? You might find it helpful to get their opinion on whether these characteristics apply to you. Then compare your answers with theirs. Have you been too easy or too hard on yourself? Just make sure you choose a friend or family member who is loving, trusting, and honest. You don't want the opinion of an uncaring or difficult person.

for you to know

Your teen years are filled with challenges and uncertainties. It's easy to get so focused on problems and disappointments that you miss the flashes of positive thoughts and feelings that break through the clouds. These bursts of positive thoughts and happiness can boost your self-confidence and energize you to face your day. But for this to happen, you have to pay attention to your spontaneous positive thinking.

If you experience a lot of anxiety or depression, you probably pay extra attention to the negative thoughts that pop into your mind. That stinking thinking is an important cause of anxiety, guilt, and other negative emotions. What if you trained yourself to pay more attention to the spontaneous positive thoughts that pop into your mind? Imagine how this could counter anxious thinking and promote feelings of happiness. Unfortunately, it's harder to concentrate on positive thoughts and feelings than on negative ones, because they don't last as long. Your positive intrusive thoughts fade so quickly, it's easy to miss them. But you can train your mind to pay more attention to positive thoughts and feelings so you're not stuck in negativity.

for you to do

Let's start with positive feelings, because they're easiest to identify. You know what it's like to feel joy, interest, gratitude, pride, love, inspiration, confidence, kindness, and the like. When you have one of these positive emotions, it's likely you are thinking of:

- A past success, love, fun, or compliment

- A creative idea or solution to a problem

- Being accepted, recognized, or loved

- Your positive personal characteristics

- Something you wish or hope for in the future

- How lucky you are, with everything you have in this life

Keeping this list in mind, think back to several times in the past when you felt happy. Write down two or three recent positive thoughts that suddenly popped into your mind during these times of happiness. For example, you interviewed for a part-time job and heard back that you got it. A positive thought might be *I must have nailed the interview. I really wanted that job. I'm going to learn some basic skills and obtain valuable work experience.*

First positive intrusive thought: _____

Second: _____

Third: _____

If you were able to come up with positive mental intrusions, great! If you couldn't think of any, don't be too concerned. You may find this next activity more helpful.

more for you to do

A happiness journal can raise your awareness of positive thoughts and feelings. Here's how it works: Look for times when you feel joy, love, pride, excitement, calm, or the like. Capture these by writing them in your Happiness Journal. (A downloadable version is available at http://www.newharbinger.com/48787.) If you have many of these experiences during the day, just write a few examples. In the first column write the date and time. In the second, briefly describe the circumstances related to feeling so positive. In the final column, write any positive thoughts, images, or memories that popped into your mind while feeling happy.

Happiness Journal

Date and Time	Where I Was, Who I Was With, What I Was Doing	Positive Intrusive Thoughts, Images, or Memories
August 15, 2021 2:30 p.m.	Alone in my bedroom, working on a new piece of music; suddenly a catchy melody came to mind.	This is great; I love it when I have a shot of inspiration. There are times when I can be creative. I know this is a gift, and it makes me feel so good about myself.

Date and Time	Where I Was, Who I Was With, What I Was Doing	Positive Intrusive Thoughts, Images, or Memories

After a couple of weeks, take a few minutes to read through your happiness journal. Are you surprised at the number of times you had positive feelings? Is there a common theme to your positive intrusive thoughts? If so, you can bring these thoughts to your mind on purpose to improve your mood. This can be an effective way to counter anxious thinking. If you had very few entries in your happiness journal, don't be discouraged. The next two activities can help you build more positive thinking into your life.

for you to know

Is your life so busy that it's hard to get everything done? Are you pulled between school, part-time work, sports, music, your friends, and then family responsibilities? When there are so many demands on your time, it's easy to ignore your positive thoughts and feelings and just focus on the anxious thoughts and feelings. But if you're ignoring your positive thoughts because you're too busy, then you're missing out on an effective method to counter your anxiety.

This next activity is especially helpful if you are often busy. It's a method you can use to slow down and pay attention to your inner thought life. It's sort of like a breathing app, which prompts you several times a day to stop and breathe calmly for one minute. This is a similar method, except the idea is to stop and think a meaningful, positive thought for one minute. I call it the *stop, think, and reflect method*.

for you to do

When we're squeezed for time, our mental health often takes a hit. It's go, go, go, with little time left to look after ourselves. You need a quick strategy that'll help you pay more attention to spontaneous positive thoughts. When a positive thought pops into your mind, you *stop* what you're doing and use the happiness journal from the previous activity to write it down. Writing in your happiness journal causes you to be more aware of the thought—that's the *think* phase of this activity. Next, spend one minute thinking more deeply about the positive thought—this is the *reflect* phase. It's very brief but will boost the effects of the positive thought. Your one-minute reflection will be more effective if you consider the following questions:

- Why did this positive thought pop into my mind? Was it because of something good I've done?

- What does this thought say about my worth and value?

- What does it say about my abilities and positive characteristics? Does it help me realize I have potential?

- Is the thought a reminder of what people like about me—that I'm accepted by them? If so, why do they like me?

- Does the positive thought suggest something about my potential or future success?

more for you to do

You'll get more benefit from this activity if you keep a record of your *stop, think, and reflect* practice sessions. You can use the following worksheet to record your practice sessions. (A downloadable version is available at http://www.newharbinger. com/48787.) Just record the date and the number of times you practiced *stop, think, and reflect* during the day. Then write down anything you learned about yourself—any conclusions you can draw from thinking more deeply about your positive thoughts.

Stop, Think, and Reflect Worksheet

Date	Number of Times Strategy Practiced	What I Learned About Myself
1.		
2.		
3.		
4.		
5.		

Practiced regularly, *stop, think, and reflect* can increase your level of happiness and self-confidence. With some slight changes in the strategy, you can use it to calm anxious thoughts. When you're feeling anxious, take two minutes to focus on your breathing. Next, recall a positive thought from your happiness journal or one you remember from practicing *stop, think, and reflect*. Consider what the positive thought means about your worth and value. You'll likely find this a useful strategy for dealing with anxious thoughts and feelings.

33 positive memories

for you to know

Memories affect our mood. How often have you chuckled, thinking back to a funny experience in the past? What about listening to a song that brings with it a good memory? Almost instantly you start to feel some of the joy and fun associated with the song. Remembering something positive can make us feel good, just as remembering a bad experience can make us feel terrible. Memories are so powerful, we can use them to change our mood and take the sting out of negative thoughts and feelings like anxiety.

There are several ways you can produce positive memories to reduce anxious feelings. You can listen to music that puts you in a good mood or look at photos that remind you of fun times and close friends. But it's not the music or photo that makes you feel better; it's the memory they trigger that affects your mood. Memories are triggered naturally most of the time, but when you're feeling anxious or depressed, it's harder to recall positive memories. The good news is, you can intentionally use good memories to feel better.

for you to do

Thinking back to an experience of joy and happiness is a great way to boost good feelings. People who are happy and confident tend to think about the positive experiences in their life. Taking the following steps helps to build positive remembering into your day and beat back anxiety and depression.

1. Make a list of photos, music, video clips, texts/comments, objects, or people that trigger memories of a positive experience.

2. Plan a quiet time—fifteen to twenty minutes without interruptions—to spend time remembering positive memories.

3. Spend several minutes listening to a positive song, looking at a photo from your list, or watching a funny video clip that recalls a positive experience. Let your mind wander, daydreaming about that pleasant memory. Focus on the part of the memory that was enjoyable—that made you feel alive or accepted. Notice how your mood changes as you concentrate on the memory.

4. Repeat the preceding steps several times a week. Make sure to use different songs, photos, and so on, so you're triggering different positive memories. If you keep thinking about the same positive memory over and over, you'll quickly get bored and it won't have a positive effect on your mood.

more for you to do

You'll get more out of positive remembering if you develop a *memory album*. Use the following worksheet to create your album, or make your own. (A downloadable version is available at http://www.newharbinger.com/48787.) List various photos, music, video clips, and so on that put you in a positive mood. Then write a very brief description of the positive memory associated with each one. You can use this list of memories when trying to think deeply about a past experience during your quiet time.

Memory Album Worksheet

Memory Cues	The Positive Memory
Photos:	
Music:	
Video Clips:	
Texts/Comments:	

Memory Cues	The Positive Memory
Objects:	
People:	

How did you do with this activity? Were you able to recall pleasant memories that made you feel some joy? Positive feelings like joy and happiness fade quickly. Your goal is not to feel a significant change, but to feel a moment of happiness that snaps you out of anxiety or depression. Then you'll need to get back to living your life. But you can do this activity as often as you like, and each time it's an opportunity to grab a ray of positive emotion. This is one more action we can use to break through the clouds of distress that can overshadow our life.

34 catching kindness

for you to know

Your day is filled with small acts of kindness, but they often go unnoticed. Your friend helps you with some difficult homework. Your kid brother gives you a compliment—for once! A teacher takes some extra time to listen to your problem, your close friend defends you when you're unfairly accused, or some people like or even add a positive comment to your latest posting. There are so many actions—some big, but many small—that demonstrate kindness. You may receive the kindness or offer it to friends, family, or even strangers.

Recognizing these acts of kindness is expressing *gratitude*. And gratitude is sweetest when we realize we did nothing to earn or deserve the kindness. It's been shown that expressing gratitude can boost positive mood and may even dampen down negative emotions like anxiety. Gratitude goes beyond just saying "thank you" to the kind person. It is a deeper understanding that another person has recognized your value and freely reached out to you, even when you didn't ask for it. The gratitude that changes our emotions has to be genuine—it has to come from your heart. It's not being grateful just because your parents say "You should be grateful for what you have."

Do you find it hard to express gratitude? Maybe you don't notice the acts of kindness you give or receive. Or you feel shy or embarrassed, so you say nothing. If for these or other reasons you are not expressing gratitude, you're missing out on an effective strategy for boosting positive feelings. And you can do something about this.

for you to do

Keeping a gratitude journal is a powerful way to become more aware of the acts of kindness shown toward you. Several times throughout the day, stop to consider whether some act of kindness was shown to you. It could be something quite small, like a friend saving a seat for you at the school cafeteria or a stranger smiling at you. Or it could be more important, like your best friend explaining how to solve a difficult algebra homework assignment.

You can use the following journal to keep track of the acts of kindness. (A downloadable version is available at http://www.newharbinger.com/48787.) The third column is not limited to acts of kindness; there you'll note anything good or positive that happened to you that day, like getting a better than expected mark on an exam or having an interesting conversation with friends.

Gratitude Journal

Date	Acts of Kindness	Good/Positive Experiences

Keep writing in your gratitude journal for a month or so. Read through it several times a week and think about the kindness shown to you. Review the third column and notice how many positive things happen. What does this say about you and your life? When you're feeling anxious or distressed, read through your gratitude journal to remind yourself that your life is not all negative and discouraging. Thinking deeply about kindness can weaken the power of anxious thinking.

more for you to do

There is another kindness activity that can boost your mood: your own efforts to show kindness to others. You know the saying "It's much better to give than receive" when it comes to gifts? We can apply this truth to our life more generally. When we are generous and giving, when we show concern for our friends, family, or even strangers, it can have a positive effect on our mood. And it doesn't have to be something big. It can be fairly small, like remembering to include your shy friend in a party invitation, or making a positive comment on someone's social media post. Start reminding yourself to do small random acts of kindness; these can help snap you out of anxiety and its stinking thinking.

the finish line

Has working through the activities in this workbook felt a little like running a race? The goal in any race is to make it to the finish line, and you have made it. Congratulations! You've taken a difficult journey with me, tackling the complicated problem of anxious thoughts and feelings. I appreciate your patience in seeing this workbook journey through to its end. I hope the time and effort you've spent with me has been well worth it.

Unfortunately, anxiety is not like a race that we can finish and forget. Anxiety is a normal human emotion, and anxious thoughts can't be forever driven from our mind. In this workbook you've learned that commonsense approaches aren't the answer for an anxious mind. And there are more effective ones: downgrading the personal significance of an anxious thought, letting go of effortful control, pulling back from assuming the worst, emphasizing your positive characteristics, and capturing moments of positive spontaneous thought. These are just a few of the workbook strategies that can transform your anxious thinking.

No doubt you've heard the expression "Rome wasn't built in a day." The same is true for dealing with an anxious mind. To be alive is to experience emotions like anxiety. So you'll need to keep practicing these strategies when it feels like your anxious mind is racing again. As new anxious concerns arise, you'll want to review this workbook and spend more time on the activities you found most helpful. You're not at the finish line when it comes to anxiety, but you're off to a very good start. Thank you for giving me the opportunity to present my approach to calming your anxious mind.

David A. Clark, PhD, is a clinical psychologist, and professor emeritus at the University of New Brunswick. He is author or coauthor of several books on depression, anxiety, and obsessive-compulsive disorder (OCD), including *The Anxiety and Worry Workbook* with Aaron T. Beck (founder of cognitive therapy), *The Anxious Thoughts Workbook*, *The Negative Thoughts Workbook*, and *Cognitive-Behavioral Therapy for OCD and Its Subtypes*. Clark is a founding fellow and trainer consultant with the Academy of Cognitive and Behavioral Therapies, and fellow of the Canadian Psychological Association. He is author of the blog, *The Runaway Mind*, on www.psychologytoday.com.

More ⏱ Instant Help Books for Teens

An Imprint of New Harbinger Publications

THE RESILIENT TEEN

10 Key Skills to Bounce Back from
Setbacks and Turn Stress into Success

978-1684035786 / US $17.95

**CONQUER NEGATIVE
THINKING FOR TEENS**

A Workbook to Break the
Nine Thought Habits That Are
Holding You Back

978-1626258891 / US $17.95

PUT YOUR WORRIES HERE

A Creative Journal for Teens
with Anxiety

978-1684032143 / US $17.95

**SOCIAL ANXIETY RELIEF
FOR TEENS**

A Step-by-Step CBT Guide to
Feel Confident and Comfortable
in Any Situation

978-1684037056 / US $16.95

**THE GROWTH MINDSET
WORKBOOK FOR TEENS**

Say Yes to Challenges,
Deal with Difficult Emotions,
and Reach Your Full Potential

978-1684035571 / US $18.95

YOUR LIFE, YOUR WAY

Acceptance and Commitment Therapy
Skills to Help Teens Manage Emotions
and Build Resilience

978-1684034659 / US $17.95

🍃 new**harbinger**publications

1-800-748-6273 / newharbinger.com

(VISA, MC, AMEX / prices subject to change without notice)

Follow Us 🔲 📘 🐦 ▶️ 📷 📌 in

Did you know there are **free tools** you can download for this book?

Free tools are things like **worksheets**, **guided meditation exercises**, and **more** that will help you get the most out of your book.

You can download free tools for this book— whether you bought or borrowed it, in any format, from any source—from the New Harbinger website. All you need is a NewHarbinger.com account. Just use the URL provided in this book to view the free tools that are available for it. Then, click on the "download" button for the free tool you want, and follow the prompts that appear to log in to your NewHarbinger.com account and download the material.

You can also save the free tools for this book to your **Free Tools Library** so you can access them again anytime, just by logging in to your account! Just look for this button on the book's free tools page.

+ Save this to my free tools library